THE
POWER
OF
ONE

THE
POWER
OF
ONE

———◆———

Sister Anne Brooks
and the *Tutwiler Clinic*

Sally Palmer Thomason
with Jean Carter Fisher

University Press of Mississippi / *Jackson*

Willie Morris Books in Memoir and Biography

The University Press of Mississippi is the scholarly publishing agency of the Mississippi Institutions of Higher Learning: Alcorn State University, Delta State University, Jackson State University, Mississippi State University, Mississippi University for Women, Mississippi Valley State University, University of Mississippi, and University of Southern Mississippi.

www.upress.state.ms.us

The University Press of Mississippi is a member
of the Association of University Presses.

First printing 2020

∞

Library of Congress Cataloging-in-Publication Data

Names: Thomason, Sally Palmer, 1959– author. | Fisher, Jean Carter, author.
Title: The power of one : Sister Anne Brooks and the Tutwiler Clinic /
Sally Palmer Thomason with Jean Carter Fisher.
Other titles: Willie Morris books in memoir and biography.
Description: Jackson : University Press of Mississippi, 2020. | Series:
Willie Morris books in memoir and biography | Includes appendices. |
Includes bibliographical references and index.
Identifiers: LCCN 2020011791 (print) | LCCN 2020011792 (ebook) | ISBN
9781496829160 (hardback) | ISBN 9781496829177 (epub) | ISBN
9781496829184 (epub) | ISBN 9781496829191 (pdf) | ISBN 9781496829153 (pdf)
Subjects: LCSH: Brooks, Anne, Sister, 1938-—Biography. | Women
physicians—Mississippi—Biography. | Osteopathic
physicians—Mississippi—Biography. | Nuns—United States—Biography. |
BISAC: BIOGRAPHY & AUTOBIOGRAPHY / Women | LCGFT: Biographies.
Classification: LCC R692 .T46 2020 (print) | LCC R692 (ebook) | DDC
610.92 [B]—dc23
LC record available at https://lccn.loc.gov/2020011791
LC ebook record available at https://lccn.loc.gov/2020011792

British Library Cataloging-in-Publication Data available

Give me a lever and a place to stand
and I will move the world.
—Archimedes

CONTENTS

PREFACE

This is a story of two opposing powers—the personal, professional, and spiritual power of Sister Anne Brooks, a dynamic Catholic nun and doctor of osteopathy, matched against the horrific power of poverty and racism in a small, dying Mississippi hamlet. Sister Anne's power is grounded in her conviction that every individual truly matters. After becoming a nun as a teenager, she taught in parochial schools for nineteen years before becoming an osteopathic physician when she was forty-three years old and was hired by the Tutwiler Medical Clinic. The clinic had been closed for five years, because no physician was willing to serve in the desperately impoverished desolation surrounding that community. But to know Anne Brooks's story is to know that Tutwiler, Mississippi, one of the poorest places in the United States, was the *place* where Anne Brooks used the *Archimedean lever* of her personal power.

She served as the clinic's medical director for thirty-four years, not only bringing health and hope to hundreds of sick and hurting individuals but also activating new energy in a dying community. Her vision brought light and healing into the darkness of lost hope. When Anne turned seventy-nine in 2017, she took down her medical shingle and moved to be with other retired nuns in the Sister of St. Joseph's Provincial House in Latham, New York. Her church and her faith are the bedrock of her existence. Yet, looking into her background, one sees this was not always so. Sister Anne's personal story took some challenging twists that might, in another life, have led to abject defeat. Her formative years certainly do not point to the woman she would become with so many accolades and awards beside her name. But for the first seventeen years of Anne Brooks's

life, her name was not Anne. Her birth name was Kathryn Vreeland
Brooks, and her family and all of her friends called her Kitty. From
1938 until 1955 she was Kathryn "Kitty" Brooks. She became Sister
Anne Eucharista Brooks when she took her Catholic vows in 1957, and
in 1982 she also became Dr. Anne Brooks, DO, when she graduated
from medical school.

The long list of Anne Brooks's accomplishments and awards is
amazing. Since the list is so varied, one is tempted to ask—who really
is Anne Brooks? Is she the soft-spoken nun who taught grammar
school for years or the effective clinic doctor who oversaw a staff that
treated close to nine hundred patients a month? Is she the sometimes
droll jokester, the charismatic fund-raiser, or the first woman chief
of staff of the Northwest Mississippi Regional Medical Center? Is
she the highly articulate trailblazer, whom local and national media,
including *60 Minutes* and *People* magazine, sought out to interview,
or the comforting presence at the bed of a sick or dying patient?

Like a kaleidoscope, her life reflects a different image at every turn.
Yet there are other facets of Anne Brooks that one does not see when
looking only at the images from her public life. The kaleidoscope
must take another turn to capture the rich, sometimes conflicted
private side that is revealed in the personal journals she shared for
the writing of this book. These journals tell of the discouragement
and wracking despair Anne felt at times but never voiced aloud.
Other, near-lyrical entries capture her probing questions, her personal
longings, and her deep faith.

Throughout this book are many, many passages using Anne
Brooks's own words lifted from her personal journals, our in-depth
interviews over this past year, dozens of newspaper and magazine
articles written about her, and the clinic's own newsletter. It is of
particular note that in all of these interviews and articles, she never
identified or referred to an individual by his or her race. In her
interactions with others, Anne Brooks related to what was beneath
the color of their skin.

In many ways this book is Anne Brooks's personal memoir. It is designed to capture her voice, her memories, and her writings enhanced and made more complete by remembrances of those who know her well or had interviewed her in the past. It is a word portrait of a truly remarkable woman whose life proves the power of one.

THE
POWER
OF
ONE

Chapter One

SETTING THE STAGE

Hope is a gift that has been given to me. I would like to pass it on. I had a need to give my life to people who needed it, a need to bring hope to people who didn't have it, to share the gift of health that I had been given, and to share my experience of God.
—Sister Anne Brooks, DO

Carl Mungenast, a self-proclaimed, practical-minded, no-nonsense businessman, is a longtime ardent supporter of Anne Brooks and her mission. He recently recalled a life-changing program he saw on *60 Minutes* nearly thirty years ago. "On Sunday evening, September 23, 1990, I was sitting in my living room in Naperville, Illinois, when a particular program caught my attention. I am not an emotional person, but Dr. Anne Brooks's words rang true. She was making the point that charity was not giving money to people but creating opportunity. She didn't believe in just giving things to people in need." Mungenast said, "I was so touched by Anne Brooks' words I immediately got up and went to my desk to write the biggest check I'd ever written to charity in my life. I was so impressed with Dr. Brooks' interpretation of what charity really means. It doesn't mean giving things to people, other than opportunity and guidance."

◆ ◆ ◆

And on that Sunday evening in 1990, millions of other people across
the nation learned about Dr. Brooks and her amazing work in Tutwiler, Mississippi. The weekly televised "newsmagazine" program
60 Minutes, with an audience of over twenty million viewers, held
the number one spot among all television programs in the Nielsen
ratings of 1990. Founded in 1968, *60 Minutes*' unique format appealed
to viewers who wanted the "real story" behind what they read in
their daily newspaper or saw on nightly TV news programs. Its
producers and reporters did their own investigations in an effort
to deliver probing, behind-the-scenes journalism, which featured
powerful personality profiles. It was a format designed to create
a strong psychological sense of intimacy between the journalist
and the viewer, a format that was highly successful. During any
given week, conversations around family dinner tables and at
workplace coffee breaks often centered on the past Sunday's *60
Minutes* featured topic.

◆ ◆ ◆

Harry Reasoner, a leading television personality at the time and one
of the original two correspondents of *60 Minutes*, had introduced
the Dr. Brooks's program with these words: "Every so often we get
a letter here at *60 Minutes* about a person so unusual or a place so
extraordinary we just have to take a look for ourselves. Well, tonight
we have a doubleheader. A doctor [Sister Anne Brooks, DO] like no
one you've ever met, in a place like none you've ever been—Tutwiler,
a principal town in Tallahatchie County, Mississippi. A place so
impoverished they call it America's third world."

◆ ◆ ◆

This was not the first time Tallahatchie County had been in the
spotlight of national and international attention. In 1955 the trial of
the murderers of Emmett Till, a fourteen-year-old black boy from

Chicago who allegedly whistled at a white woman, was held five miles south of Tutwiler in the small town of Sumner in the Tallahatchie County Courthouse. After a five-day trial, an all-white jury found the accused, Roy Bryant and J. W. Milam, not guilty. Four months later, protected by double jeopardy laws, Bryant and Milam confessed in an article in *Look* magazine to the brutal murder that left Till's face mutilated beyond recognition. National and international newspapers reported outrage at the Emmett Till verdict and harshly criticized the racist social conditions in the Mississippi Delta. When his body was delivered back in Chicago, Till's mother, Mamie Till Bradley, channeled her rage by insisting on an open casket at his funeral and welcomed photographs. She wanted to show the world the horrible reality of intractable racism. Pictures of Emmett Till's butchered face appeared in magazine and newspaper articles across the nation. Fourteen hundred miles north of Tutwiler, the publicity of Till's murder made an indelible impression on a seventeen-year-old postulate who had just entered a Catholic convent in Rome, New York—the future Dr. Brooks.

◆ ◆ ◆

Now, in 1990, Reasoner in his *60 Minutes* broadcast reported that the town of Tutwiler, located in the heart of the Mississippi Delta, "was a region so economically devastated that Congress had declared it the poorest place in America." After World War II, as agriculture became mechanized, much of the rich Delta land was purchased by large corporations that replaced thousands of sharecroppers and field hands in the area with machines. Gainful employment was hard to find for those who had been "replaced." There was more malnutrition and disease in the Tutwiler area than found in third world countries. More babies died before their first birthday than in Panama or Haiti or Mexico. The infant mortality rate was twenty-three deaths per one thousand births—more than twice the national average. One-fifth of the babies born in Tutwiler were born to teenage mothers—twice the national average. Poverty and illiteracy among the black population were endemic. Unemployment was rampant. Although civil rights legislation and government, religious, and philanthropic programs battled against the pernicious legacy of the rigid segregation of the Jim Crow culture, racism and a strong resistance to integration were still very much in evidence.

Reasoner reported, when a task force of doctors surveyed the area in the late 1980s, they "found people as close to the brink of survival as one is likely to find in this country. In the town of Tutwiler, located in the heart of the Delta, the shanties that many of the black folks lived in were far below substandard."

Many of the shanties that Dr. Brooks's patients called home were perched on the Hopson Bayou that runs through the center of Tut-wiler. Flooding of the bayou was a major problem. Twenty percent of the homes lacked indoor plumbing, and raw sewage was routinely dumped from slop jars into the bayou's waters, which overflowed two or three times a year. At least six to eight inches of water annually seeped into those homes along the Hopson Bayou—some homes got twelve inches of water three times a year, with raw sewage in that water. And when the waters receded, filth and dead animals were left behind.

A few blocks away from Hopson Bayou, little remained of what used to be the small, bustling downtown of Tutwiler, Mississippi. When E. B. Seymore was interviewed on the 1990 *60 Minutes* broadcast, her voice was full of nostalgia as she remembered when Tutwiler was the shopping and entertainment hub for most of Tallahatchie County. "This was a thriving little town. On Saturday afternoons, my mother-in-law used to love to sit in the truck and watch the people go by. She just enjoyed that so much. There were two theaters and a drugstore . . . four dry goods stores, four grocery stores, a barbershop, a pool hall. We had it all."

Others, who also grew up in Tutwiler, remember that in those early days there were two sides of town—the black side and the white side—literally separated by the railroad tracks and racial segregation.

◆ ◆ ◆

When Dr. Brooks arrived to reopen the medical clinic in Tutwiler in 1983, she was challenged by Tutwiler's grinding poverty. This was the type of place she had been looking for—the type of place where she could be of real service. The clinic that was built by federal dollars in the 1960s had been abandoned, shuttered for over five years. Dr. Brooks settled in and brought her wondrous, holistic—some said revolutionary—approach to health care to Tutwiler.

Several years after she had become established at the clinic, the postmaster of Tutwiler, Melvin Browning, said, "We've had a couple of doctors come in, and they'd stay a year or so, and then they'd pack up and leave. I've seen doctors come and go, but I've never seen anyone like Dr. Brooks. She goes around making house calls. I know of lives she's saved. They wouldn't have got to the hospital if she hadn't gone to their house and given them the first aid they needed."

Anne Brooks said, "I see in my patients this enormous struggle just to survive. It makes me in awe of them. If a person is economically poorly off, they are so busy surviving that health actually doesn't hold a very important place. They are too busy trying to eat, trying to find food, possibly trying to even find a place to live." When she arrived in 1983, Dr. Brooks saw women who had never had a Pap smear or a breast exam, a man who couldn't read the instructions on a prescription, fourteen-year-old girls who were pregnant for their second time, and malnourished babies who were fed nothing but soda pop and potato chips.

Reflecting back on her first few months in Tutwiler, Dr. Brooks said the situation was so horrible she was energized by the rage she felt but had to swallow. But gradually, realizing that rage does not solve problems, her emotions made a dramatic turnabout. She stopped being angry. "I think I was able to reach past the anger and look at a person, and if that person was hurting, I'd like to help." Care and a heartfelt compassion for the whole person, while seeking to implement a practical solution for the horrific, seemingly unsolvable problems an individual faced, became her signature style. As far as Dr. Brooks is concerned, "It's not enough to treat someone just as a medical patient. Probably the most important thing in medical care is to empower patients."

When Dr. Brooks arrived in Tutwiler to open the abandoned clinic, the first thing she did was to tear down the wall separating the black and white waiting rooms. The color of a person's skin made absolutely no difference to her. "I look at the person. I don't look at the disease. I look at the whole person. . . . When you talk about the whole person, you talk about their water supply, the roof over their head, how they treat their children, how their children treat them. When someone comes in and says, 'I've cut my leg,' I say, well, how did you cut your leg? They say, 'Well, I fell through the porch.' The next thing I say is well, how can we fix that porch?"

From the very beginning Anne Brooks's vision and dedication attracted other likeminded nuns to help turn the Tutwiler Clinic into something much more than a doctor's office and to find ways to bring that impoverished town back to life. Dedicated to taking care of the "whole" person, Tutwiler Clinic became the town's hub for a variety of social services, so needed and appreciated that eventually these "non-medical" services expanded into a full-blown community center with its own building.

◆ ◆ ◆

Genether Spurlock, a retired schoolteacher and the first black woman to serve as mayor of Tutwiler, now serves as a program director at the Tutwiler Community Center. When asked about Anne Brooks, she responded, "What did Dr. Brooks mean to this town? She was our . . . how can I put it? She was an angel to us. She really was. She brought so much to this town. The town was on the verge of—you know, I probably would have been gone if things hadn't changed.

There was a great migration—everybody was just leaving, 'cause there was nothing to do. But she kinda just saved us. . . . Dr. Brooks, you can ask anyone in town. She was our guardian angel—we depended on her for so much."

Chapter Two

ANNE'S BEGINNING

I am much of what my parents and especially my grandparents were.
—Wallace Stegner

In exploring a bit of Anne (Kitty) Brooks's background, one finds that there is a strong strain of intellectual, academic, and economic accomplishment. How in the world did Anne Brooks end up in what Harry Reasoner had said was "a place so impoverished they call it America's third world—Tutwiler, Mississippi"? Her father's family had deep roots in the cultural/social/professional network of nineteenth-century New England. Her great-grandfather Francis Augustus Brooks was a corporate attorney and railroad president in Boston. His son Morgan Brooks, who was Kitty's grandfather, was a noted inventor, a nationally known professor of electrical engineering, and a successful businessman. He and his wife, Frona Marie, had nine children. Frona Marie was born in France and held a rare distinction for a woman of her era. She was a college graduate, having graduated from Smith College in 1883.

Anne's maternal grandfather, Julius Goebel, born in Frankfurt am Main, Germany, had begun his illustrious academic career before he immigrated to the United States in 1885. During the next forty years, Professor Goebel taught at Stanford (where future president Herbert Hoover was his student), Harvard, Johns Hopkins, and the University of Illinois in Urbana. He was an author who corresponded with Otto von Bismarck, the chancellor of the German Empire, and was considered one of the foremost Germanic-language scholars in America. Also a poet, a leading authority on Goethe, he cofounded the Modern Language Association. He and his wife, Kathryn Vreeland Goebel, had seven children.

One of those seven children was Anne Brooks's future mother, Anchen (who changed her name to Anne) Vreeland Goebel. Both Anchen and Roger (Anne's future father) grew up in Urbana, Illinois. They both attended Urbana High School and the University of Illinois, where both of their fathers taught. Two years older than Anne (Anchen), Roger was a corporal in the university's signal drill team during his sophomore year at the university in 1917. The United States entered World War I that year, and Roger Brooks, according to the university yearbook, with patriotic fervor wanted to become a *real* military man. He received an appointment to the US Naval Academy at Annapolis, which he entered in 1918 and graduated as a commissioned officer in 1920.

With a known future and a regular paycheck, Roger asked for his high school sweetheart's hand in marriage. On March 20, 1921, surrounded by family and friends, Anne (Anchen) Goebel and Roger Brooks were married in Urbana, Illinois. Although armistice had been declared shortly after Roger had entered the academy as a plebe, the United States Navy continued to patrol the world and monitor local trouble spots, which meant that, as with many "military" marriages, Roger and Anne (Anchen) would not settle into a traditional married life. Over the next ten years, the young couple were separated and lived apart most of the time. Roger served aboard various ships in various oceans, while Anne made her home base in Urbana close to her family and childhood and college friends.

The couple did, however, have an extensive, rather disjointed, delayed honeymoon in several foreign countries in the spring of 1923. *To go to Turkey to visit my husband* was the reason Anne gave when applying for the passport she received on November 14, 1922. She and Roger also visited Egypt, Spain, and Italy on that trip, and she embarked from Naples to arrive back in New York on July 31, 1923. During the next five years Anne and Roger arranged to meet at different spots, close to a port of interest, whenever he had leave time. But at the start of the new decade, their lives changed dramatically.

In 1930 Roger received an onshore, stateside assignment at the Naval Department in Washington, DC. He and Anne moved to the nation's capital, rented an apartment in the heart of the city, and for the first time since their wedding day settled into the daily routines of a typical married life. Their first and only child, Kathryn Vreeland Brooks, whom they called Kitty, was born on June 4, 1938. Anne was forty and Roger forty-one—they had been married seventeen years.

Their lives, once again, changed dramatically three years later, after the Japanese bombed Pearl Harbor on December 7, 1941, and Germany and the Axis powers declared war on the United States of America. Roger, now a naval captain, was called to active duty and assigned to Admiral Halsey's fleet in the Pacific. This separation was to have serious implications for their family. Before leaving, Roger moved his wife and three-year-old Kitty into a small, two storied, Cape Cod–style house on Livingston Street in a quiet, family-friendly neighborhood in Chevy Chase, Maryland—a move that was to isolate Kitty's mother.

Sister Anne remembers her many fun times as a young girl living on Livingston Street—going trick-or-treating on Halloween with other neighborhood children and playing hide-and-go-seek and kick-the-can in the summer evenings. However, she noted that her mother always rang a bell when it was time for her to come home from her evening of play in the street with the other kids on her block; she remarked, "No other parent ever rang a bell. But I really didn't know any of the other parents. I was forbidden to go home with any of the girls on my block, because they were Catholic, and most of the families on my block were Catholic." Kitty's parents, both extremely anti-Catholic, made it very clear that they and their young daughter were not to become too friendly with those of that religion. For that matter, any type of religious practice was not a part of young Kitty's life. She was pretty much a loner when she was in grammar school. Neighborhood kids were not welcome in her house.

Yet Kitty had her secret. One of those Catholic girls, Sally Attig, who lived across the street, became her best friend. Together they climbed the trees that flanked Kitty's front yard. And in spite of her mother's edict, when her mother wasn't looking, Kitty would sneak over to Sally's house to play in her backyard. In her own house, little to no affection was shared with her mother. Kitty shared meals with her mother but remembers that even as a young child she did not want to be in the same room with her. She was offended by the smell of her mother's cigarettes and avoided contact with her as much as possible. It was not a happy household.

Kitty started kindergarten in 1943, at the Sidwell Friends School, the grammar school she attended until the middle of the sixth grade. Sidwell is a prestigious, highly selective, Quaker school located in Washington, DC, that has educated the children of many notable politicians, including the children of several past presidents. The Obama, Clinton, and Nixon girls, and Theodore Roosevelt's son, were educated at Sidwell. A school bus from Sidwell picked Kitty up in front of her house every morning and brought her home every afternoon, so her mother didn't have to drive. In fact, Kitty was not sure if her mother knew how to drive.

Remembering those days, Sister Anne said, "When I got off the school bus every afternoon and went into the house, I tried to avoid my mother's welcoming kiss and hug. All saturated with cigarette smoke, she smelled terrible."

◆ ◆ ◆

Presumably, children at the Quaker school, not being Catholic, were welcome in the Brooks home in those years. One of Sister Anne's vivid memories is when she was in the third grade, her mother asked her to invite some of her classmates from school to her birthday party. She noticed before any of her friends arrived that there were several men in dark suits snooping around their backyard. She never knew which of her guests required such monitored protection.

On Saturdays, when she was in the fifth grade, Kitty often walked the couple of blocks to Connecticut Avenue with the girls in her neighborhood to get ice cream cones and "check out" the pretty things in the shop windows. One store they would visit several times in an afternoon had a machine that took an x-ray of their feet inside their shoes. Fascinated by the ability to see through leather and skin, they always took pictures of their feet four or five times in an afternoon.

Sister Anne recounted her lasting memory from one of those Saturday afternoons: "I saw several women, a couple of blocks away, dressed in black with white halo sort of things on their heads and asked the other girls who they were and why they were wearing such strange outfits."

"Oh," her friend Sally said. "They're nuns."

"What are nuns?" Kitty asked, never having heard the word before.

One of the other girls giggled and whispered, "They're teachers, and they keep babies in the basement!"

"I felt a chill run down my back," Sister Anne recalled. "What do you mean in the basement?"

"I don't know," the friend answered.

Sister Anne continued: "No one said another word, but we all walked a little faster and hurried back to the shoe store to look at our feet again. Then one of the girls said, 'I gotta go home now,' and left. Without another word the other girls quietly dispersed, and from that day forward, I could never get the episode out of my mind. I kept it a secret, never asked anyone about it."

◆ ◆ ◆

During those war years in Chevy Chase, Kitty's mother had little to no social life and rarely left their house. She had grown up in a large family of four sisters and two brothers. As a university coed with close friends, a gaggle of sorority sisters, and an active social life, she had always been surrounded by people with similar interests and backgrounds. Even in her first decade of marriage, when she and Roger were separated for long periods of time, she lived in Urbana, close to her parents and college and childhood friends.

All of Kitty's thirteen aunts and uncles had survived into adulthood—two brothers and four sisters on her mother's side plus her father's three brothers and four sisters—but none lived in the Washington, DC, area, and all were presumably caught up in their own lives during the war. The only relative Sister Anne remembers well is her Aunt Mimi, who lived in Philadelphia and "sent . . . fancy tins of gourmet British food at Christmas every year." Ten years older than Kitty's mother, Aunt Mimi felt a special bond with and responsibility for her younger sister. She was deeply concerned about Anne, since she was now so alone and consumed with anxiety over Roger, who was at war on a battleship in the Pacific.

With no close friends, few acquaintances, no family nearby, and her husband at war on the other side of the world, Kitty's mother spent her days and nights alone, with her growing daughter. She had "big" dreams for her daughter. When Kitty was only three years old, her mother enrolled her for future entry in Sweet Briar College in Virginia. And having herself cherished the social whirl enjoyed by a young lady from a prominent family with strong social connections, she most likely dreamed about the time Kitty would make her debut. But who knows what Kitty's mother dreamed for herself, or if those dreams she once held for herself had been completely dashed. In later years, the most distinct memory her daughter held of her mother when they lived in Chevy Chase was, "Mom spent her days at home, sitting in the study, smoking, listening to the radio, and drinking her whiskey out of a green glass."

Chapter Three

A CHANGE IN DIRECTION

The more we let God take us over, the more truly ourselves we become.
—C. S. Lewis

One summer evening in 1949, Kitty sat at the top of the stairs, emotionally paralyzed as she listened to her mother's hate-filled screams, punctuated by the sound of slaps on bare skin and breaking glass. Was her mother throwing glasses? Kitty was in the sixth grade, and her family was still living in their house on Livingston Street in Chevy Chase, Maryland. Her dad, a captain in the navy, had come home from fighting the "Japs" (her mother's word) about four years before and was still in the navy, working at the Navy Yard. For the last couple of months, he and her mother had horrible, explosive fights almost every night after Kitty had gone upstairs—presumably to go to bed.

She couldn't understand what had happened. When her father first came home from the war, it had been wonderful. Her mother seemed so happy. He was jovial and full of love. When Kitty told him her dollhouse needed some stairs, she later found him in the basement building tiny little steps in her dollhouse. Sometimes on Saturday she would drive with him down to his work at the Washington naval yard and gun factory, where he was responsible for naval ordnance. She would talk with his secretary while he was off inspecting "this and that." One Saturday he took her ice skating with his lady friend named Janet. Kitty remembered ice skating was fun, but she didn't tell her mom about Janet.

On her tenth birthday she got the best present she had ever received—a black and white cocker spaniel puppy named Freckles. Kitty loved her puppy. She said, "It was like the little sister I never had." She now had a confidant with whom she could share her life. Very early, on most Saturday mornings, with Freckles on leash, she would hop on her bike and ride down to the corner bakery for a "yummy" cinnamon sweet roll, hot out of the oven. It was good to get out of the growing tension in the house.

Now sitting, listening to the rage coming from below, she held Freckles close to muffle her sobs. She wanted to run away—didn't care where she went, she just wanted to get away from the nightly fights and her mother's screams. Miserable and deeply confused, Kitty shook her head and took a deep breath. Where would she go? Where could she go? Giving Freckles an extra-hard squeeze, she felt her puppy's cold nose turned up to her cheek as he licked away the tears.

A few weeks later Kitty's answer came. One evening when her mom was cooking supper in the kitchen with the door closed, Kitty was in the study, sitting on the floor while her dad sat in the lounge chair beside his desk. He looked over at his daughter, snuffed out his cigarette, took a deep breath, and said, "Kitty, I'm going to leave your mother."

She could hardly believe his words. Quickly scooting across the room, she plopped down in front of his chair, and wrapped her arms around his legs. "Oh, Daddy, PLEASE take me with you." Scattershot words tumbled out as she tried to tell her father how her life was unbelievably terrible . . . how awful she felt . . . her mother screaming at him every night . . . she wanted to run away . . . knew she must . . . but where . . . how . . .

Roger Brooks listened, shook his head, and sighed. He understood. His daughter was miserable. He was being transferred. Could he take Kitty with him? If he didn't, would she become the target for his wife's rage that he had been experiencing for months? Placing his hands on his eleven-year-old daughter's shoulders and gripping them tight, Roger Brooks took a deep breath and said, "Your mom has an appointment with the hairdresser in a couple of days to get a permanent. That'll take about three hours that she'll be out of the house. I can come home, get what you want to take, and pick you up at school."

"What about Freckles . . . we have to take Freckles."

"Kitty, you put all the stuff you want to take in the bottom drawer of your dresser and I'll come home, get Freckles, grab your bottom drawer, and come pick you up, and we'll leave town."

Flooded with relief, Kitty started to cry, but Roger quickly pulled her face to his chest and said, "Shush, Kitty, you don't want your Mom to hear you."

Years later Sister Anne learned that her father had also grabbed all the money out of her parents' joint bank account.

◆ ◆ ◆

Father, daughter, and dog drove for three days heading south. They stayed in motels at night and ate at truck stops during the day until they reached Key West, Florida, where there was a large navy base. Kitty had never seen the ocean. Everything was so very different, so new, so exciting—the vast expanse of water, the palm trees, the banana trees, the huge ships docked at the naval base.

Roger was going to live in the BOQ (bachelor officers' quarters), and he had to find a place for his daughter to live and attend school. First thing on the morning after they arrived, Roger, although he was deeply suspicious of Catholics, took Kitty to the Convent of Mary Immaculate boarding school to apply for admittance. Back home, Kitty had been forbidden to play with Catholic children—a rule she found ways to circumvent. The convent was a large three-story building with a long, wide porch encircling its outside to provide access to the rooms inside, because there were no interior hallways. It was a stark, foreboding, institutional-looking building—so very different from the large, elegant old mansion surrounded by beautifully landscaped grounds that Kitty had known as a student at Sidwell. Stepping up on the porch, Kitty and her father found the door marked Admissions and entered a sparsely decorated office with a large mahogany desk in its center. A nameplate on the desk read—Principal-Sister Delphine Marie.

As Sister Marie rose to greet Kitty and Roger, Kitty felt more than "a little scared." Remembering the nuns she had seen at a distance in Chevy Chase, this was the first nun she had ever seen up close, and the sight made a lasting impression on the young girl. Years later, after her name had been changed from Kitty to Sister Anne Eucharista, she wrote, "Sister Delphine Marie had black bushy eyebrows, was wearing a kind of a white sunbonnet sort-of thing on her head with a black veil that went down her back. There was a short black cape from her neck to her waist and a very large six-inch metal cross with an image of a body on it, which hung from a cord around her neck. Her black dress came all the way to the floor . . . with sleeves that went all the way to her fingertips." Kitty could not stop staring, until Sister Marie smiled at her, which made her feel a little better.

There was room for Kitty in the sixth grade, but she would have to take an entrance exam that would last three days. Kitty took the exam and passed easily. She didn't think it was very hard. On the third day of testing, she finished early and was waiting for her father to come pick her up, when Sister Marie took her out on the porch and pointed to the library door. When Kitty opened that door, she saw another nun, this one with a blue apron over her black dress, leaning on a dust mop.

"What kind of stories do you like to read?" asked this nun.

"Oh, horse stories, mystery stories . . ." Kitty replied. The Sister went over to a shelf and said, "I have just the book for you," and handed Kitty a book entitled *Murder in the Nunnery*. Stunned, Kitty couldn't wait to read it. Remembering that Saturday morning, when she was in the fifth grade and encountered her first nun, she thought that she might at last be able to find out about those babies in the basement.

◆ ◆ ◆

When Roger arrived at the convent in mid-afternoon on that third day, Sister Marie told him that Kitty had passed the entrance exam with "flying colors" and would skip seventh grade. She could move into the dormitory that very evening and start eighth grade classes the next day. Roger and Sister Marie went to the library to tell Kitty the good news, and when she asked about Freckles, Sister Marie said he could stay outside, on a long rope tied to the porch by the kitchen. Roger and Kitty made a quick run to the motel where they had been staying to get Freckles and her belongings; they returned to the convent before supper. Kitty said goodbye to her father and moved into the dormitory in time to go to evening vespers and dinner with the other boarders.

The dormitory with thirty-six beds was built above the school auditorium. Each bed had long curtains hanging from metal rods attached to poles at the bed's four corners, which were pulled for privacy. Next to each bed was a metal stand with a drawer and a couple of shelves, plus every boarder had a locker at the end of the dorm room. Hastily stashing her clothes in her assigned locker, Kitty took a slow look around, shook her head, and swallowed hard, wanting to squash her mounting apprehensions. It was so very different from the cozy, pink and white bedroom she'd known all of her life, the bedroom she'd never shared with another soul, except Freckles.

When Kitty crawled into bed that first night, she pulled the curtains closed tight around her. This was the first time in her life she had ever slept in a room with anyone but a member of her family. Everything was so very different, so very strange, and she was so very tired. Fortunately, she quickly fell into deep slumber. Kitty Brooks had entered into a reality so unlike anything she had ever known. A reality she would find totally foreign, puzzling, with moments of sheer terror—at other times, pleasant, intriguing, even inspiring. A world governed by strict scheduling and established rules, yet infused

by an atmosphere of calm knowing and loving care—an atmosphere
so very different from what she had known at home.

◆ ◆ ◆

When the wake-up bell rang very early the next morning, the other
girls were eager to tell Kitty what she must do. She got up, hurried
to the lavatory, washed up, and quickly dressed. When one of her
new roommates handed her a beanie, she looked puzzled and was
told that "a female must always cover her head when entering a
church sanctuary." Not understanding but compliant, Kitty put on
the beanie, lined up to go down the outside iron stairs, and walked
across the campus to the church in silence behind two nuns at the
front of the line.

Never before had Kitty been inside a church or chapel. Her irre-
ligious parents had never spoken of God. At Sidwell in the Quaker
tradition, which was never explained to Kitty, students were taken
into a large plain room and instructed to sit quietly with their own
thoughts. In those times Kitty remembered she had thought about
what the other girls were wearing or what she might do after school.
Now she entered a Catholic chapel for the first time: "It was a big room
with lots of benches and a long small board in front of the bench that
had padding, so you could kneel on it. In just a few minutes a man
dressed in beautiful, embroidered clothes came in and stood in front
of a marble table with his back to us. A young boy dressed in a black
robe with a white filmy shirt stood there with him. At one point the
man held a white round thing up in the air, and the boy rang a hand
bell. I poked the girl next to me and whispered, 'What's that white
thing that guy is holding up?' 'Oh, that's God,' she whispered back.
'How can that be God?' I said, having no idea who God was or what
God looked like. 'I don't know' she whispered back, 'But it's God.' That
was sure a mysterious thing."

Kitty was completely baffled by the strange new world she had
entered.

After the service the girls walked to the dining hall for breakfast and then to their classroom. One of the girls showed Kitty to a desk and got her a textbook. The teacher, a nun standing at the front of the room, told the class to open their books to chapter 6. When Kitty followed those instructions, she was confronted by "an awful picture—the whole page was gray, and there was a wooden cross, a big one, and hanging on it was a man with thorns on his head and nails in his hands.

"I couldn't look at it. It was too scary and bloody." She turned to the girl in the next row to ask, "Who's that?"

"Oh, that's God," the girl said.

"How can that be God?" Kitty whispered.

"Shh!" Kitty looked back at the page, gave a shudder, and closed her eyes.

At the end of class, the students again lined up to go to lunch. On entering the dining hall, one of the girls pulled Kitty aside to show her how to "spy on the nuns." Kitty peeped through a hole in a wall of old paneling and watched as the nuns entered their dining room on the other side of the wall. With their hands in their sleeves, they each bowed to a cross with a figure on it, hanging on the wall at the far end of the room. Kitty thought this was incredibly strange behavior and became increasingly confused and concerned. She wanted to know what all this was about but was afraid to ask any more questions. And not wanting to cause trouble, she fell into the convent's daily routine and followed the rules—went to chapel, went to class, played at free time with Freckles tied to his long rope by the kitchen, and sometimes played with the other girls. But she was increasingly uncertain where all this was going to lead.

Yet, very slowly, she began to realize that the nuns had a special way of teaching her about the things that were so confusing—so scary. One morning after breakfast one of the nuns asked Kitty if she would help her with the dishes she was washing. Kitty joined her at the sink, and the nun began to talk about God—who He was and where she could find Him. Kitty listened carefully, because of her curiosity about that round white thing the priest held up in church and the picture of the man on the cross. Her classmates had called both of those things "God." Gradually Kitty understood that the nun was teaching her Catholic catechism—the summary of the principles of Christian religion in the form of questions and answers, used for the instruction of Catholics: *Who is God? God is the Supreme Being who made all things and keeps them in existence.*

Sister Anne remembered that one Saturday the nun took her up to the chapel on the second floor of the school. "She taught me that God lived in the gold box on the marble table that was called the altar. And I learned that when the big candle that was burning in a large red glass vase was lit, Jesus was there and I could talk to Him. And that talking to Jesus was like talking to a friend, and that was called prayer. He could answer my questions by talking to my heart."

Kitty felt like her mind was bursting! This was all so new, all so strange, but it all felt so wonderful. As the days, and then weeks, passed, she made friends with a lot of the girls, and the classes became easier. She was beginning to love this school and the nuns, who were always kind and sometimes helped her groom Freckles because there were prickly things on the grass, called sand spurs, that kept getting caught in his furry coat and tail. Kitty was delighted when on another Saturday morning a nun asked her to help clean the chapel. She now understood that it was good to clean the house of God. In fact, she wrote later, "I realized I loved God and knew He loved me, too. I loved to go sit in the chapel when we had break times, to think and say a prayer I had learned, which began, Our Father . . . and wait for God to talk to my heart."

When she had arrived at the convent, the nuns, "all wrapped up and dressed in black," had terrified Kitty. "It turned out that they were absolutely wonderful people, who insisted that my mother was good, and that my father was good. Of course, I didn't believe them, because when you're a teenager in the middle of a separation, you hate both parents," who always fought.

One morning, after Kitty had been at Mary Immaculate for almost six weeks, she pushed open the door of a stall in the lavatory to see one of her favorite nuns cleaning the toilet.

"Sister Anne, what are you doing? You shouldn't have to do that."

"No, Kitty, you are wrong. In God's eyes there are no demeaning tasks. Keeping our world clean and healthy is our sacred duty."

It was in that moment that eleven-year-old Kathryn Vreeland Brooks made a decision. She knew she wanted to become a nun. She wanted to be a part of this dedicated, caring, love-filled family—so very different from anything she had ever known.

Chapter Four

BREAKING AWAY

Only I can change my life. No one can do it for me.
—Carol Burnett

In the spring of 1950, during her eighth grade at the convent school in Florida, Kitty and Freckles usually headed for the beach very early on Saturday mornings. She loved to watch the rising sun turn everything pink, even the battleships moored in the bay, and after a brief jog along the sand and a survey of the fishermen's catch off the pier, she would spread out an old army blanket and sit to watch the gathering crowd of beachcombers. One morning in mid-April she noticed a large man in a dark business suit, a tie, and cordovan street shoes walking toward her. Kitty knew he didn't belong. Stopping and standing over her, he said, "Hello, young lady. Could I ask you your name?"

"Kitty Brooks. Why do you want to know?"

"Your mother has sent me to find you. She wants you to come home."

Quickly gathering her things and calling to Freckles, Kitty cried, "No, I won't go," and raced for a safe haven. The man did not follow or try to stop her. She never saw him again, but that afternoon her father came to the school to say that he and her mother were getting a divorce. Kitty would need to come to the hearing that was in three weeks in a court in Florida.

◆ ◆ ◆

The day was sultry, hot as twelve-year-old Kitty entered the courtroom and saw her mother for the first time in almost nine months. Aunt Mimi was with her, and the two sisters sat, stoically grim-faced. Her mother continued to nod assent to the terms of separation, until the judge asked, "Have you and Mr. Brooks agreed upon the living/ visitation arrangements for your daughter Kathryn?"

They had not. The previously modulated tones of her parents changed rapidly into loud accusatory shouts. But their spite-filled words were cut short with a curt rap of the judge's gavel. "Let's ask Kitty what she would like." With the judge's question, Kitty realized for the first time in her life, she might have the power to get what she wanted.

Her father had said he wanted her to live with him and go to Key West High School, a place she'd heard had a terrible reputation for drugs and "fast-loose living," And, too, he was going to marry his girlfriend, Janet, as soon as his divorce was final. Kitty couldn't stand Janet. Soon after she and her father had moved to Florida, that bossy woman had arrived in Key West, rented a beach bungalow, and completely taken over her father's life, acting like she had the right to dictate Kitty's every move. She felt her life would be ruined if she lived with that woman and went to Key West High School. Even though her mother was drunk most of the time, Kitty would have more say over her own life, and she would be back in her old neighborhood.

Kitty took a deep breath, stood up, and with a pounding heart told the judge she wanted to move back to Chevy Chase to live with her mother and attend the Academy of the Holy Names. Her wonderful friend Sally Attig, who lived across the street, was starting high school at the Academy of the Holy Names in the fall. Having skipped seventh grade, Kitty would also be ready to start high school in September. That was what Kitty wanted, and that is what the judge ordered.

Young, twelve-year-old Kitty, in stating what she wanted, had given no thought to how or who would pay the tuition. She had been told that neither of her parents could or would pay the tuition for her to attend the Academy of Holy Names.

◆ ◆ ◆

That summer Kitty moved back to Chevy Chase to live with her mother. Once again back in her old neighborhood, Kitty went with Sally out to the Academy of the Holy Names several times. She was certain that this was where she wanted to go to high school but uncertain how to apply or to somehow get her parents to agree. Summer school was in session, and on one of her visits she saw Sister Joan, a favorite teacher from her convent school in Florida, coming out of a classroom. Seeing someone she knew, loved, and trusted, Kitty excitedly ran to Sister Joan and, learning that she was now a teacher at the academy, asked her what she should do. Kitty told her that her heart was set on attending Holy Names and that she was absolutely sure she wanted to be a nun but that her parents couldn't or wouldn't pay the tuition.

That afternoon Sister Joan contacted Father Carl Lyon at the Church of the Blessed Sacrament in Chevy Chase, the parish church close to where Kitty lived, to tell him about this exceptionally bright young girl who wanted to dedicate her life to the Church's mission. Father Lyon agreed to give Kitty the necessary instruction for her to become a Catholic, and he, too, was soon impressed with her bright aptitude and devotional commitment. Learning that her parents were unwilling or unable to pay her tuition, he arranged for the Church to fund Kitty's full tuition for her high school education at the Academy of the Holy Names.

The Monday after Labor Day in 1951, Kathryn Vreeland Brooks entered the Academy of Holy Names, the all-girl, Catholic college-preparatory high school, located in Silver Springs, Maryland. Every morning she and Sally Attig caught the city bus at the stop on Connecticut Avenue, a block away from their homes, and transferred two times before reaching Silver Springs, where they alighted and walked fifteen minutes across an empty field to school.

On the Saturday evening of September 29, 1951, Kitty was baptized at the Church of the Blessed Sacrament in Chevy Chase. Since she had no white dress, she wore her white school uniform. The next morning she took her first Communion. Sally's father, Francis J. Attig, and Sally's mother, Helen Attig, were her godparents.

Kitty was once again living with her mother and felt emotionally isolated. Her mother carried out her daily tasks in a fog of quiet desperation, with all of her hopes for any possibility of a meaningful relationship, a normal, even happy life dashed. She remained mute most of the time—her violent words had been spent. Over the next four years, the Attigs became a very important part of Kitty's life. She found refuge and strength in her new faith by crossing the street every evening to participate in the Attigs' daily family rosary. She believed that her mother never missed her. Never knew where she had gone. Having just become a Catholic, Kitty was "taken by the beauty of the repetitive devotion and the meaning of it. It was so very important for me to make sure I was over there at their house when it was time to go ahead and do the family rosary."

As soon as Mr. Attig arrived home from work, the family—Sally, her invalid brother, and her mother and father—and Kitty would gather in the living room to kneel down on the carpet to pray together by repeating the rosary. Kneeling together helped her engage totally in her prayers, and she found strength "in the ability to say repetitious words because you didn't have to wonder what you were supposed to say next, you just said the next words and the next words and the next words . . . your mind might be wondering if Jimmy liked Brenda, but you couldn't say anything but the words of the prayer." And they were words she was memorizing during her instruction with Father Lyon—the Apostles Creed, the Lord's Prayer, Hail Mary, Hail Holy Queen—words that were of profound significance in the development of this young girl's spiritual life.

Sally's father, who led the group, often gave a specific reason for their prayers—help for a friend or colleague who was sick or had a major problem, sometimes guidance on a burning national issue—so their prayers often focused well beyond the immediate concerns of those gathered in the Attigs' living room. This made a lasting impression on young Kitty: "In a way, we participated in a tiny, tiny bit in someone else's troubles. And because we had the power of prayer, it gave us something to do for somebody else who was having trouble."

Mr. Attig not only gave spiritual guidance to his daughter and goddaughter, but as the official reporter of debates on the floor of the US Senate, he exposed them to the world of Washington politics. He was responsible for the written record of the United State Senate from the 1950s to the 1970s. When a particularly important debate occurred, he encouraged the girls to be eyewitnesses to the making of history. One prominent event that made a lasting impression on Kitty was attending the Senate's infamous McCarthy hearings with Sally in their junior year of high school. There Kitty witnessed that vitriolic words and unsubstantiated accusations are incredibly destructive to an individual's life. This was a lesson that helped shape the adult character of Anne Brooks.

◆ ◆ ◆

Kitty's four years of high school were a balancing act between commitment and avoidance. Committed to her spiritual growth and her studies, Kitty was up before six o'clock every morning to ride her bike the seven blocks to early Mass at Father Lyon's Church of the Blessed Sacrament before hurrying home to put her bike away and catch the bus to get to school. By attending summer school she was able to pursue her studies the year round. Although she ate and slept at home, Kitty spent very little time in her own house and avoided, as much as possible, any close contact with her mother. She said that her mother "smelled terrible, always puffing on a cigarette. It was so awful, I did not want to get sick, and I considered that a sickness."

During her senior year in high school, Kitty noticed her mother was increasingly withdrawn, eating less and less but still sipping from her ever-present tumbler of whiskey. And then one morning, as Kitty scurried to get to morning Mass, she heard moaning behind the closed door to her mother's bedroom. Pushing the door open, she saw her semiconscious mother sprawled on the floor beside her bed with one arm at a weird angle. Kitty rushed to phone Dr. Billy, their family doctor, and he told her to get an ambulance and take her mother to the Wisconsin Avenue Outpatient Clinic, about a half a mile from their house.

The ambulance came. The attendants rushed upstairs and loaded her mother onto the stretcher. Kitty watched them struggle to turn the corner on the stairs' narrow landing as they rushed down the stairs, then place the patient in the rear of the ambulance. Following closely behind, Kitty pulled the front door of the house shut and, before the rear doors of the ambulance were closed, climbed in to sit beside her mother, who was now coughing and screaming and pointing at the dark hinges in the otherwise all-white walls inside the ambulance. "Get those goddamned cockroaches out of here."

Her mother was delivered to the clinic, and after she was examined there, she was sent down to the City Hospital to be admitted for extended care. Kitty again rode in the ambulance with her now nearly comatose mother and remembers that it was a very long trip, into the depths of downtown, into a part of the city where she had never been. When they got to the hospital, sixteen-year-old Kitty was responsible for filling out the paperwork. When it came to the question about religion, Kitty wrote, "If she has a problem, call a priest."

Three nights later her mother's condition deteriorated. The staff member called for a priest from the nearby downtown church in Washington, DC. The priest came to Kitty's mother's bedside and anointed her before she died. At three o'clock in the morning, Kitty answered the phone to learn that her mother was dead. In relating this part of her story, Sister Anne made no further comment.

Kitty moved in with the Attigs while the Brooks house stood locked, except when she went across the street to get clothes she needed. Although Kitty didn't want to talk with her father, wasn't even sure where he was or if he knew her mother had died, she knew something must be done about the house. Father Lyon understood and arranged for a lawyer named Mr. Cromady to tell Kitty what to do. Mr. Cromady told her to take an inventory of everything in the house, which she did. "I remember going up into the attic and seeing my mother's steamer trunk. Her wedding dress was in it. And then his stuff—his cutlass and part of several versions of his uniform. I think he had five different uniforms at one time, depending on what was going on. I had to bring all that stuff down. But I didn't bring everything down. There were a thousand cockroaches swarming, and some of them were falling from the ceiling and getting under my shirt. I couldn't stand cockroaches."

Her mother's final hallucinations in the ambulance had been of cockroaches. Kitty probably realized that during those many years of her mother's loneliness and despair, she must have climbed those attic stairs to find those cherished remnants from her happier times, repulsively infested with millions of horrible little insects—such a terrible image.

Now, soon to be starting a new life, Kitty wanted no further contact with anything associated with her mother and father. She was committed to becoming a sister of the Church—her "new family." Kitty asked Mr. Cromady and Mrs. Attig to arrange for the items from the attic to be given to charity or taken to the nearest dump.

◆ ◆ ◆

On Kitty's high school graduation day, all the seniors, fluttering around in their caps and gowns and high heels, were lining up outside St. Michael's Church. She said, "I saw this guy leaning against a pillar in the church, and I wondered who it was. And as I got closer, I realized it was my father. His hair was white, and his skin was yellow, and I panicked." Kitty had not seen her father since the divorce court in Florida, four years before. She broke out of line and ran to find Sister Joan. "My father's here and I'm afraid he will take me away." Sister Joan nodded and said, "Don't worry, Kitty, I'll take care of it. Now, you'd best return to your place in line."

As the graduates filed out of the church after the ceremony, Sister Joan invited Kitty and her father to the priests' dining room behind the convent for a visit and something to eat. Kitty's father accepted the invitation but said he couldn't eat anything, because he had colon cancer. After the three were seated and a few pleasantries exchanged, he turned to Kitty and said, "Come on, I'll pick you up and take you home." Without hesitation Kitty declared, "No. I don't want to go. I'm going to enter the convent."

"You're what?"

"I'm going to enter the convent in July."

Her father looked at Kitty and said, "No, you are not."

Gathering her courage she looked directly at him, and in a voice as calm as she could manage, Kitty reminded her father of something he had once said to her: "When something is the matter, you work to find some way to fix it."

Sister Joan sat quietly watching father and daughter argue, each diametrically opposed to the other's position, until Kitty's father slowly shook his head and said, "Well, Kitty, you can try it."

Chapter Five

STRUGGLES IN THE CONVENT

In humility, I decided to apply myself with my whole soul . . . to
abandon myself in complete confidence.
—Fr. Jean C. J. D'Elbée, July 2, 1955, Silver Springs, Maryland

Seventeen-year-old Kitty Brooks was at least two inches taller than
but just as nervous as the other eleven young women who stood
waiting on the near-empty platform at the railroad station in Silver
Springs, Maryland. The freshness of the early summer morning
seemed to soften the voices of well-wishing, tearful parents and
sleepy younger siblings, who were saying their good-byes, giving
hugs and, in some cases, a final request or heretofore forgotten
word of advice. These twelve young women were recent graduates
of the Academy of the Holy Names. The year before each one had
individually applied to become a postulant in the Community of the
Sisters of the Holy Names, which required the assent of her parents.
Before her mother died Kitty had asked her; she had said, "OK, if
that's what you want to do." She had also written to her father but
deliberately sent her request to the wrong address. Knowing he was
obstinately opposed to Catholicism, she didn't want him to receive
her letter. When her application was being reviewed, she was asked
about her father's consent. She said, "I wrote for his permission but
never received an answer." Thankful for her little bit of subterfuge,
she knew that she'd been right when, to her surprise, her father had

shown up at her graduation and voiced his strong disapproval of her becoming a nun.

Kitty and the other eleven applicants had each received a personal letter of acceptance from the Provincial Superior. Now they were all on their way to enter the order's convent. Even before their graduation from high school, they had packed their trunks and taken them to their school gymnasium to be sent ahead to the convent in Rome, New York. The novitiates already in training at the convent would unpack and put away those belongings.

Kitty could hardly believe that this day was finally here. For the past five years, becoming a nun had been the driving force of her every waking hour. But now, on her big day—the beginning of her new life—she felt confused, overwhelmed by the magnitude of her decision. She was scared.

Turning to Sally and Mrs. Attig, her surrogate family, who had brought her to the station, Kitty wrapped her arms around each in turn but was at a loss for words. The Attigs had been her emotional, spiritual support for so long, like family, even though she had lived with them only during the last six months—ever since her mother's death. She then knelt down to grasp Freckles behind the ears, trying hard to staunch her tears. Her goodbye to Freckles, her most steadfast companion, may have been the hardest good-bye of all, even though she knew he had a good home with the Attigs. Kitty picked up her small train-satchel and ran to board the train, all the while waving to those she was leaving behind.

How different her new life would be. She had no idea where it would lead. She only knew it would be a safe haven, a blessed commitment, a total contrast from the circumstances and situation into which she was born seventeen years before. She would even receive a different name—that is, if she could prove herself worthy. She had decided to sever all connections with her father and all of her relatives.

◆ ◆ ◆

July 5, 1955, is a day forever emblazoned in Kitty's memory. When the train pulled into the small station in Rome, New York, shortly after 5:00 p.m., several automobiles were waiting to take the new postulants to the convent. It had been a long day, and with only a sack lunch of a sandwich, a cookie, and an apple, the restless, hungry girls were anxious to be on their way. After being greeted by the local drivers, they eagerly piled into the waiting cars and drove about fifteen minutes through gently rolling hills to a large building with two dark staircases that circled up on each side to the main entrance. Stepping out of the car, Kitty looked up to see a nun in a long, black habit standing on every step of the two staircases. She had never before seen this many nuns in one place. Taken aback by such a dramatic introduction to her chosen life, she muttered to herself, "Oh, my God, what did I get into?"

When Kitty reached the landing at the top of the stairs, the novitiate who had been assigned as her guide introduced herself and took Kitty inside, up another flight of stairs into a dormitory room. She was shown the single bed where she would sleep, surrounded by curtains hanging from poles attached at each corner of the bed. When her guide took her to a bank of closets at the end of the long room and pointed to one, Kitty was surprised to see that her trunk had been unpacked. "All my clothes were right where they were supposed to be." Her novitiate guide reached for a long black dress hanging alongside Kitty's clothes and told her to change into her new attire. Putting on a black dress was the first step for a postulant entering the convent. After Kitty quickly made the change, her guide showed her how to put on her veil. She then explained the convent's daily schedule of prayer, meal times, classes, and recreation, giving special emphasis on the most basic cardinal rule—a postulant must keep silent at all times. She must never talk except during the time called recreation, a short time after lunch or supper.

A ban on talking? Kitty was so full of questions and thought it "terribly stupid," but she said nothing. She ate her supper and went to bed her first day in the convent without saying another word. "I just sort of shut up and did what I was supposed to do. . . . I would only talk during a time called recreation . . . that was it."

The no-talking time was about twelve hours every day, which meant no conversation or words were to be initiated by the novitiate. First thing every morning, right after the postulants got up, they . . . [hurriedly dressed] and were led in prayer for about a half an hour before they went to Mass, and then they went to breakfast. You didn't talk at breakfast, because you were still thinking about [what had been said in] church. There was no conversation during any meal. However, those first few months there was a reading table where the new postulants were alphabetically assigned to read, usually something from the *Lives of the Saints*. So, we didn't talk during the meals—we listened to the readings. There were twelve people at a table, and after we finished eating, a dishpan was brought to the table. One person got the dishpan, two people got towels to dry the dishes, and then they passed the dishes to others to stack. Whoever had kitchen duty came to take the dishpan away, and the table was set for the next meal. . . . You didn't talk in class either, unless, of course, you had a question for the teacher. That went on for a couple of months.

In time the specific rules, exacting schedule, and dress code began to make perfect sense to Kitty. When asked in later years about the dress code, after a nun's dress requirements had changed, she mused, "I think it's the same reason you wear a swimsuit when you go swimming. If you are going to be a swimmer, you dress like a swimmer. If you are going to be a nun, you dress like a nun. . . . I think having a specific dress helps to keep your mind where it should be. If you are dressed in a black dress and you are on your way to church, then you had much greater reason to take part in a prayer situation rather than just jabber with your neighbor. And keeping your mind where it should be is keeping your mind focused on God, focused on someone who needs prayer. . . . Having a specific dress means you begin to believe what part of your life you are living. . . . I think in the beginning part as a postulant, you were basically trying to find out who you were."

Kitty got caught up in her studies—the prescribed courses of Bible and the history and role of the Catholic Church, plus Jewish studies, and studies of other religions, as well as challenging, college-level extension courses from Bonaventure University. She had to learn how to chant, say the psalms with others in unison, and recite specific responses to questions like: "How do you behave if you are going to become a Christian?" Or, "If you want to be prayerful, how would you learn the prayers?" The postulants were continually tested and took many exams that were graded.

After about ten weeks, Kitty and the other new girls completed their postulancy and were ready to become novitiates, receive their holy habits, the proper dress of their religious community, and their new names. This was a big church ceremony presided over by the bishop. Each postulant in turn, with a candle in her hand, would kneel in front of the bishop in his full regalia, and hear him say her secular name and then declare her religious name. This represented the life-changing step of becoming a novitiate in the religious community of her choice. Weeks before, each postulant had submitted three names for the provincial council to choose one as her new name.

On the big day, as the postulants, eager to learn their new names, lined up to be singularly presented to the bishop, the postulant in front of Kitty was particularly nervous. She had asked for her brother's name, but in her heart doubted she would be allowed a masculine name. As she knelt before the bishop, ready to respond "Deo gratias" (Thanks be to God) to his pronouncement, she couldn't contain her excitement when the bishop said, "In the future you will no longer be called Carol Anne but Sister Kevin Michael." The newly entitled Sister Kevin Michael was so thrilled she unconsciously jerked her hand with the candle in it, and hot wax flew all over the front of the bishop's liturgical vestments. Kitty could barely stifle her laughter as she stepped forward and knelt to hear the bishop solemnly pronounce her religious name, "Sister Anne Eucharista." Sister Anne was ecstatic. "I was floating on air." This was the name she wanted.

Eucharista, one of the names Sister Anne had chosen, is the ancient Greek name for the Blessed Sacrament in the Roman Catholic Church, sometimes called Holy Communion or the Lord's Supper. The Church honors the Eucharist as one of her most exalted mysteries—the blessed mystery where Jesus Christ is truly present. The bread and wine of the holy sacrament of Communion inexplicably become his body and blood.

Although Anne feels that words can never fully capture her feelings, she speaks of her inexpressible gratitude for the unconditional love she experienced when she opened her heart to Jesus. In gratitude for God's love, she wanted to dedicate her life to God. She wanted Jesus to always be intimately with her, always be a part of her life. "It's a bizarre experience of receiving God into my heart. I can't explain it . . . I just feel it . . . know it." Through the miracle of the Eucharist, God's reality became a part of Sister Anne and continues to feed her soul to this day.

When asked why she chose Anne as her new name, she responded, "Good question." It was the name of her mother, of whom she had disdainful, horrible memories.

Somehow, the difficulty I had with her in my lifetime was erased. I don't know how that happened. It was just gone. So when I had a chance to honor her, in spite of her constant smoking, in spite of her drunkenness all the time, it seemed right for me to be Anne. I wasn't sure I loved my mother. She was very difficult. She was always smoking. She always smelled terrible . . . I hated to kiss her and then I wouldn't. . . . I didn't think Mom was good for much. . . . She and my father cussed. I thought she hated my father. They always had fights. . . . She was always sitting in the corner in her rocking chair drinking whiskey. So how could I show her I loved her? I didn't know and I think the reason I chose Anne was to say . . . "Yeah, Mom, I really did love you." . . . That's what I think. It just somehow came out . . .

When you are in a religious community, you are taking on the responsibility of continuing what you have been taught.

Forgiveness and love are fundamentals in her now dedicated
religious life. Honor your mother is one of its Commandments.

◆ ◆ ◆

Anne described what happened after each of the postulates had
received her new name. "We then each went into the sacristy, where
we dressed in our holy habits and were given a white veil of the rank
of a novitiate. And after our studies, in two years we would make our
first vows of poverty, celibacy, and obedience, again in front of the
bishop, and change our white veil for one of black. We would then be
sent *on mission* to teach in one of the community's schools."

These young women were stepping into a time-honored tradition.
The wearing of a nun's habit dates back to the very earliest Christian
communities in Roman times. During the second and third centuries
CE, women, usually virgins or widows, who called themselves "Brides
of Christ" wore veils and coarse "habits" to show the world that they
had vowed to lead a religious life in community with other women
of like mind and heart. During the next two centuries, nuns became
increasingly organized, and the Church sanctioned the building of
convents as a place for these dedicated, chaste Christian women to
live and support each other. Some lived wholly within the walls of
the convent in a life of consecrated prayer and contemplation, and
others journeyed outside the convent's walls as apostles to the poor
and the sick. Nuns, both within and outside the convent, always wore
their habits.

◆ ◆ ◆

During her first year at the convent, Anne started having problems
with enormous, near-constant physical pain. She had developed severe

rheumatoid arthritis. It got to the point that she couldn't climb the stairs up to the classrooms, and her knees became so red, painful, and swollen she couldn't kneel. The doctor gave her knees cortisone injections every week and told her to take ten aspirin four times a day. She said, "A couple of times they hauled me off to the hospital for treatment. I was getting scared that if I needed treatment for something they were calling arthritis, they might send me home. And that was a terrible feeling. . . . I would talk with the Mother Superior, and she would say, 'If you don't want to go home, just say so.'"

Anne was torn. She had no reason to want to go home. For that matter, where was home for her? But she didn't want to be a drain on the community if she had a disease and was incapable of keeping up her studies and the required routine. Filled with doubt, her days were increasingly filled with questions. "Do I have to go to the hospital? Do I have to get medicine? What happens with something like this?" As she asked these questions to those in charge, she began to realize that sometimes they didn't know either. "Does the doctor know? Does the Mother Superior have the answers?" There were far too many questions that didn't seem to have an answer.

◆ ◆ ◆

At first, if it was a pretty day when the others were outside playing during recreation, Anne would sit in a chair under a tree beside the large field of grass but would not participate in any of the ongoing sports. However, not only did her knees hurt, she soon found it was too emotionally painful to see the others enjoying tossing balls, playing tag, and rowing boats on the small pond—activities she longed to do. So, she usually stayed inside reading or studying in the back of the chapel. She later recalled, "I lived with the fear that I won't be able to make it. If I can't walk now, when I am a teacher, I won't be able to write on the blackboard. If I can't stand and sing with the others, how am I going to get my ordination? There was so much to learn. When I couldn't climb the stairs to the classroom, they would tell me to take aspirin. So I took aspirin as I was told . . . I didn't want to miss anything. . . . Even if I couldn't climb the stairs to the classroom, I would study my head off."

With her frequent visits to the doctors and occasional hospital stays, Anne became increasingly terrified of being sent home. Yet she always felt, "Since I'd gotten this far, do you think I'm going to leave on my own?" And she would pray "like crazy . . . OK, God if you really want me to keep going, you are going to have to fix it."

◆ ◆ ◆

In spite of her pain, through determination and commitment, Anne persevered. The convent's arduous routine—rigorous study and exacting schedule—lasted another two years, until the novitiates were ready to become full-fledged nuns. In Anne's words:

> You've learned all the Church's teachings and the ability to put into your head the reality of divine love and what it is like. And you've learned how you keep track of things in your life . . . [that will] allow that love to improve yourself. How you put in your life the reality of who God is for you. God is not just a picture on the wall. God is someone who cares very deeply about you. There is a need for each of us to understand our relationship with God—not the God of the "holy" part, but the [personal] God that cares about us. . . . And the reality of this is truly knowing that God is always caring about us. That is kind of heavy-duty stuff. It's not something you study about one night and have a test on Monday. It's not like that at all. You go through your whole life as a Sister, worrying about God and how God loves you. And how you love God. . . . The reality of God's love for us is a humdinger.

Chapter Six

THE TEACHER LEARNS

You don't become a nun to run away from life. . . . It's not because you've lost something, but because you've found something.
—*The Bells of St. Mary's*

Sister Anne made her final vows within the Order of the Holy Names of Jesus and Mary in late spring of 1957 and was assigned to teach fifth grade in a primary school for girls in Tampa, Florida. She looked forward to this assignment—her calling. In trying to describe her commitment to serve, she often said, "It's really hard to explain. What you feel is beyond words." Even though she was told she would be on crutches and in a wheelchair the rest of her life, Sister Anne was very grateful for her place in the rich tradition of her Church's response to human need. She identified deeply with its mission and its history. In 1727 the Sisters of the Order of Saint Ursula in New Orleans had founded the oldest continually operating school for females in the United States. It was a free school that offered classes to female African American slaves, free women of color, and Native Americans.

Sister Anne's Order of the Holy Names of Jesus and Mary, founded in Canada in 1843, had the same commitment to the education and personal development of young women. At that time, almost no Canadian women had any control outside their homes, except for the nuns of the Roman Catholic Church. In this French-speaking colony (later province) of Quebec, dozens of independent religious orders of nuns specializing in works of charity had been created. These Catholic orders were an influential and powerful part of French Canadian society from its beginnings.

Even so, up until the mid-nineteenth century, formal education for females was extremely limited, usually not extending beyond religious instruction and skills such as needlework. Education for intellectual and/or career development was reserved for and offered only to the young male population. Sister Marie-Rose (Eulalie Durocher), a Catholic nun from Longueuil, Quebec, appalled by such partiality, took action and persuaded the church fathers to sanction the founding of the Order of the Holy Names (Sister Anne's order) "to educate the poor, to empower struggling young women both spiritually and intellectually, and enable those within her influence to develop their full potential."

The Order of the Holy Names of Jesus and Mary rapidly expanded its mission, fostering schools and convents across Canada and into the United States. Its reputation grew and in 1868 the bishop of Florida sent a request to the order in Montreal to send five nuns from their convent to open a school for girls and to form a convent in Key West. Five sisters from Montreal went to Key West and opened the first and longest-running Catholic School in the state of Florida. This was the school where almost a century later, eleven-year-old Kitty Brooks found a welcoming, safe haven of love that changed her life.

And in 1879 two sisters went from the convent in Key West to open a two-room schoolhouse in a blacksmith shop in Tampa. A small beginning that grew into a thriving primary school for girls, where seventy-eight years later, in 1957, Sister Anne Eucharista Brooks arrived to teach fifth grade at the Academy of the Holy Names, her first teaching assignment.

◆ ◆ ◆

Sister Anne adapted easily to her new role in life as a teacher, even though she was increasingly challenged by wracking pain in her ankles and knees while standing. She spent most of her hours at school in her wheelchair. Sister Anne loved the children, and they loved her. She presented her lessons in a patient, no-nonsense, challenging yet supportive, often fun manner that let the ten-year-olds know she cared and could relate to them at their level. One of her students, recovering from crashing through a glass door the previous year, was also in a wheelchair. It became a game every morning after chapel for teacher and pupil to race their wheelchairs down the hall to see who could make it first to their classroom.

On her first summer vacation, wanting to strengthen her teaching skills and increase her knowledge about her new profession, Sister Anne started working toward a bachelor of science in elementary education at Barry University, a private Catholic university in Miami, Florida. Because of her growing health issues, it took twelve years for her to receive her degree, cum laude, in 1970.

◆ ◆ ◆

Ever since Sister Anne had started training to be a teacher, she had received weekly cortisone shots in her knees, but "no one made a definite diagnosis, and it [the pain] never really calmed down." Finally, a doctor in Tampa diagnosed her problem as arthritis and told her, "You are going to die *with* it, not *from* it. So, this is what you have to do. You may not teach a full day, you have to use a wheelchair, and I want you to rest in bed half of the day and take your medicine [forty aspirin a day]."

At the conclusion of her second year of teaching in Tampa, the Mother Superior, wanting to help lessen or cure Anne's pain, arranged to have her sent to Dr. Goldsmith, a rheumatoid arthritis specialist at the Peter Bent Brigham Hospital in Boston, which had been founded in 1914, to serve patients with arthritis and other debilitating joint disease. Anne had three months of inpatient hospital care before she was sent to intensive rehabilitation at the Robert Breck Brigham Hospital. She laughed as she remembered that part of her physical rehabilitation was spending her days "making a chair in the carpentry shop and listening to the soundtrack from the *Sound of Music* all day long, since they didn't know what type of music to play for a nun. I would have much preferred some Beethoven and Bach. To continue my exercise without being in the hospital, they sent me to help with the cleaning at a convent focused on rescuing 'the ladies of the night.' I was then assigned to teach fifth grade for a spring semester in the Immaculate Conception School in New Bedford, Massachusetts, and then a summer remedial reading program at the St. Thomas School in Albany, New York."

After a year in the Northeast, wearing a back brace but not solely reliant on the wheelchair, Sister Anne returned to Florida in the fall of 1961, to teach for four years at the small San Pablo School in Marathon Shores. In 1965 she was again summoned to Tampa to be the principal and teach the seventh and eighth grades at St. Peter Claver School, a segregated school for black students only. While at this inner-city school, she was again reliant on her wheelchair, and every morning after early Mass at the church, the pastor would help her get in his car, pack the wheelchair in the back, and take her to school. Because there were steps into the school building, he kept a folded lunchroom table just inside the door and would put it on the steps as a ramp and push her up this very steep slope.

Once inside the building she faced the constant challenge of getting up to the auditorium on the second floor. However, her seventh-grade boys solved that problem. They would carry her up the steps in her wheelchair and say, "Now, Sister, if you don't give me an 'A,' I'm going to drop you." Anne's voice filled with nostalgia as she remembered, "They were great kids. I loved them. Ricky has a job right now at Cape Canaveral. I'm so proud of him."

Sister Anne had her own methods of disciplining unruly students. One day she got a note from a first-grade teacher saying, "I have a child who is not nice. Will you please help her get better?" Those were the days when Sister Anne still wore her full, black religious habit. She went down the hall to the classroom, drew herself up to her full height of five feet, eight inches, and stood tall in the doorway—a formidable sight. In a firm, no-nonsense voice she asked, "Suzy, will you come with me?" Wide-eyed Suzy reluctantly got up from her desk and shuffled slowly into the hall. Before going to the classroom, Sister Anne had gone into the little lunchroom where there was a copy machine and turned it on to make a loud, kar-plunk, kar-plunk, kar-plunk noise. Now, standing in the hall outside the lunchroom, she said to little Suzy, "Your teacher says that you were bad, that you were making trouble. Do you hear that sound—kar-plunk, kar-plunk, kar-plunk? That's a spanking machine. Do I have to take you into that room?" Suzy's dark eyes shot open as she spun around to run back to her classroom. The teacher reported that Suzy was very good for the rest of the day.

One day at St. Peter Claver School, Mark Levine, an eighth-grader, came running into Sister Anne's office and said, "Sister, lock the gates. Do it. Lock the gates." The gates separated the school building from the rectory, the little house where the priest lived. The telephone was in the rectory. There was no telephone in the school, and she had no intention of locking the gates, which would separate her from the phone. Recalling how she got up to go outside with Mark, she said, "I did not see myself climbing over the fence to use the telephone, but I suddenly realized it was very quiet. Dead silence. Something was terribly wrong." Sister Anne locked the gates.

There was always a low level of sound, a lot of laughter, and loud music here and there from the "honky-tonk" district a block away from the school, but not a sound on that day. Sister Anne learned later that three Klansmen in business suits had that day walked slowly down the full length of the district in the middle of the street, while the black shop owners quietly stood in their doorways with their arms folded. "Nothing happened. Nobody spit, nobody cussed—they just stood there and watched. They did nothing but stand there. . . . About a week later the guys [white-supremacist toughs] came over from Orlando and started the race riots in Tampa. At that point [the violence became so bad] the priest had to leave, and they closed the school. They were putting the wounded on the rectory's porch that was behind the school, but they [the rioters] didn't touch the school. They set fire and burned down the laundry behind the school, but they didn't touch the school. The school was totally fine, but the Church returned it to the government [the city's public school district]."

When the school closed Sister Anne was transferred to a very wealthy parish in Clearwater:

> The poverty in the inner city is something I had really worked for, to get the kids up to grade level, to get them where they needed to be so they could get a job. When you get to Clear Water, they have their boats, they have their skis, they have all this stuff. Their poverty is the love of their parents. . . . Pop was over there, mom was over there, kids came home and nobody home. So, they grabbed whatever was in the icebox. So their poverty was love. I was teaching seventh grade, so I would hang out at school, and they would come up with a conversation and ask me, "What do you do when Joe Blow starts making passes at me? What do you do when you get an F on your paper? How do you come up with an excuse when you are late for class?" Well, anyway, it was that sort of culture. . . . It was during that time I saw an ad in the paper—FREE CLINIC OPENING. It was then that I volunteered after school to see what I could help with.

Chapter Seven

PAIN, RECOVERY, AND NEW BEGINNINGS

The practice of medicine to me is wanting to communicate God's love.
—Sister Anne Brooks

The free medical clinic that advertised for volunteers was in St. Petersburg, about a forty-minute drive from Clearwater, where Sister Anne was teaching, and the convent where she lived. With a burning desire to help those trapped in poverty, largely because of the color of their skin, Anne signed on to be a volunteer at the clinic. Every afternoon after class at St. Cecilia and on weekends, she drove to St. Petersburg to answer the free clinic's phone and, since she knew how to type, help with their record keeping. She liked being there. She liked the patients, and they liked her. She liked the other volunteers who willingly gave their expertise without pay—the doctors, the nurses, the paramedics, the counselors, a couple of street priests. There were others like Butch Anderson, a disillusioned veteran of the Vietnam War, who lent his brawn to moving furniture and assisting crippled patients in need of a strong arm and lent his heart to those needing a word of encouragement or comfort. Dick Allen, one of the priests, "spent his days and evenings hanging out with the kids on the streets . . . was so much fun and became a special friend. He was so gentle and so genteel."

After about a year as a volunteer, Sister Anne was asked to become the clinic's full-time, modestly paid director. She contacted her Mother Superior requesting permission to leave her teaching position to become the full-time director of the St. Petersburg free medical clinic. When word went through the informational channels in the Catholic organization, she received a call from Bishop McLaughlin: "Sister Anne, you can't accept the offer as director of that free clinic."

"Why not?"

"They might pass out birth control pills."

In spite of the bishop's words, Sister Anne accepted the offer and was enthusiastically befriended and supported by the street and parish priests in the clinic's neighborhood. She recalled the time, soon after she had started as the full-time director, when Dick Allen came in with his pocket full of bills of various denominations. The night before, the bishop had called a meeting of all the priests in the diocese and, suspicious of the clinic's birth control policies, said that they [as leaders of the Church] must not give any financial support to the clinic. The priests were seated around a big round table, and as the bishop spoke, those bills had been passed under the table to Dick Allen to take to Sister Anne.

Although she arranged to live with another nun in a garage apartment behind the clinic, Sister Anne kept her room at the convent. She wanted to maintain the close spiritual as well as physical connections with her religious order and life. She served as the clinic's director for four years, from 1973 to 1977, and later declared, "It was one of the most rewarding things of my life—the Gospel came alive and I saw God."

Marcia Biddleman, who worked with Sister Anne from 1974 to 1976 and was the executive director of the St. Petersburg Free Clinic through the 1980s, recalled Sister Anne's dedication. "She always had very strong convictions about not getting bogged down with anything other than service to the people who needed help. Her interest in medicine was quite phenomenal. She was always asking the doctors questions and had an amazing ability to remember medical terms.

Driving her was just an anger over how many people didn't have medical care." Biddleman went on to comment on one of Sister Anne's most delightful attributes: "Sister Brooks has a good sense of fun, but her fun is being around people and seeing them get better. It's an absolute dedication."

◆ ◆ ◆

John Upledger, one of the volunteer doctors, had a regular osteopathic medical practice in town during the day and was at the clinic almost every evening. "Medicare and Medicaid had just started, and he refused to accept Medicare or Medicaid in his private practice. When someone who couldn't pay for medical services came to see him at his office, he sent them to the free clinic, where he would take care of them after his daytime office hours." Sister Anne has a vivid memory of the evening when she first met Dr. Upledger. "I was leaning against the wall while he examined a patient, and he looked up at me to ask, 'Why are you leaning up against the door jamb?'"

She responded, "Because I hurt."

"Why do you hurt?"

"Because I have arthritis."

"Oh, I can fix that."

"Oh, sure, I know about you doctors. I just spent six months in Boston."

Upledger's tone became insistent. "Look, I just came from an acupuncture course and ..." Sister Anne felt her body go rigid as she turned away and shook her head, her inner voice silently shouting, "Forget that. No way. I mean, No Way." The doctor shrugged his shoulders, saying, "No rush. Think about it. I'm not going anywhere."

Anne did think about it. While wearing her back brace, she was always in excruciating pain, and for years it had been impossible for her to take even three steps on the stairs. Over the next few weeks, she could think or pray of little else other than Dr. Upledger's recommendation. "I began to get it in my head, maybe I should try it. What

he explained is that our body has channels of energy that come and
go, but if you have pain, the energy in this particular [energy] avenue
becomes very busy dealing with that pain. What you want to do is
open up that channel and let the pain out. You open the bottom of
the channel and let it out, and for the pain to have someplace to go,
you open up another channel. I was fascinated by the whole idea, but
I wasn't very interested [in having acupuncture done on me]. . . . But
. . . I decided to try it and went to see him at his office one afternoon
about three weeks later."

Before scheduling her visit to his office, Sister Anne did her
research—as was her practice. She learned as much about osteopathic
medicine, Dr. Upledger's specialty, as she could. She discovered that
in addition to the standard training for a doctor of medicine (MD),
a doctor of osteopathy (DO) received extra training in manipulation
of the musculoskeletal system—the body's interconnected system of
nerves, muscles, and bones that makes up two-thirds of a person's
body mass. They had a holistic approach to medicine—a "treat the
whole person" approach to health care, believing that patients are
more than just the sum of their body parts. Sister Anne's research
revealed that DOs were trained to use their ears as well as their hands
and listen carefully to all of the concerns of their patients in order to
help them develop attitudes and lifestyles that didn't just fight illness
but helped prevent it.

Anne went to see John Upledger at his office. "He treated me many,
many times and never charged me. [On that first visit,] he had me
take off the back brace that reached from my neck to my tail . . . the
doctors in Boston said it was supposed to help my back . . . so he could
work on my back and use acupuncture. It felt good." On subsequent
visits, "he also did lots of other stuff besides acupuncture—nutrition,
general medical and osteopathic treatments. Eventually, I needed
manipulation under anesthesia because of the contractions I had
developed from being in and out of a wheelchair or on crutches
for seventeen years. I was finally taken out of my back brace . . . for
good." Anne had arranged for a street priest who worked with her at

the clinic, to drive her "home" to the convent after that appointment. When she arrived everyone at the convent was in bed, but since the doctor had told her that she would be pain free, she remembers saying to herself, "I think I'll go upstairs, even though I slept downstairs. I went up stairs, and I didn't hurt. I was pain free . . . WHOOPEE! . . . So. I went down again, went to bed, and slept like a log.

"John Upledger, DO, was the only one of many physicians—including one who wanted to do a total hip replacement when I was only thirty-three—who insisted I could get better. Through osteopathic manipulation and acupuncture I could beat the arthritis, correct my scoliosis [diagnosed years before by the specialists in Boston], and relieve my joint pain, so as to be able to begin to move my contracted muscles."

Instead of just treating Anne's specific symptoms, he concentrated on treating her whole body and nurturing her confidence that she could help herself through a new understanding of how the mind, body, and spirit are deeply connected. Rather than focusing only on the pathology at the site of her pain, he worked to activate the deep interconnections of her body through osteopathic manipulation, a technique that every DO (doctor of osteopathy) learns in med school. This manipulation is based on the idea that tightness and restriction in one's nerves and muscles can be caused by or lead to other problems. So DOs are trained to use their hands to gently move a patient's joints and tissues to correct any restrictions in his or her range of motion. The doctor also "worked" on Sister Anne's mind through honest revelations about her past treatments and current health, plus a strong dose of supportive encouragement.

Shortly after she began her weekly visits with Dr. Upledger, Sister Anne recalled, "I can still see him seated on the windowsill in the hospital one January day in 1975, telling me my blood test was highly suspicious for leukemia. Naturally, it was pretty scary, and it was only a year later that he was willing to say it had been due to all the drugs I had been given during those eighteen years." Sister Anne did not have leukemia. "He treated me gratis every week for two and a half years, with the result that after eighteen years of wheelchairs, crutches, cane, and back brace, I was finally pain free."

Dr. Upledger also had Sister Anne change the habit she wore. "I had always worn a veil, so in a way I had no identity as a person. I think my unhappy childhood and the subsequent repressed life I led probably contributed to the stress that caused the arthritis." Nearing her fortieth birthday, Sister Anne Eucharista Brooks was beginning to feel a new kind of personal freedom she never before had experienced. All the while John Upledger was seeing Sister Anne, she said, "He was pushing me to become a doctor, saying, 'You can be a doctor for free since your tuition would be paid through the National Health Service Corps.' And I would say, 'I don't want to be a doctor. I'm a teacher. I work with inner-city kids . . . how I love those kids . . . besides I could never pass chemistry and I'm almost forty years old.' So whenever he began talking to me about being a doctor, I'd say you are crazy, John. Here I am a teacher, of kids who are needy.' But John continued to push."

"And then I began to wonder, is this a call from God? You know, when you are a nun you are waiting to hear what the Lord is going to say. Sometimes it's a glaring holler at you. But I wasn't sure about this one. But with John continually urging, I decided to go to night school to see if I could pass chemistry." She felt "lost at first and it was nearly a disaster," but with "a lot of help from other students," and using her skills of organizing information and presenting it clearly, Sister Anne got an A in chemistry. "So, then, the key was—will my religious community allow me to do this? Because when you are in a religious community, you go where you are sent, you teach what you are taught . . . all that kind of stuff. I wasn't sure how to sort this out."

She was at a crossroads and knew that the direction for her life was a decision between her and God.

◆ ◆ ◆

Becoming a doctor would be a radical change in Sister Anne's life. But the Catholic Church was in the midst of a radical historical change.

In 1959, two years after Sister Anne had entered her teaching career, Pope John XXIII announced the creation of the Second Vatican Council, saying that it was time to "open the windows [of the Church] and let in some fresh air." The Pope's leadership, his words, would have tremendous implications for the role and status of nuns. For more than two thousand years, they had lived and operated within the highly hierarchical, institutionalized patriarchy of the Roman Catholic Church. This was about to change. By the middle of the twentieth century, seismic changes occurred in the larger society concerning the role of women.

After the Second Vatican Council, which convened in 1962 and lasted until 1965, the way members of the world's largest Christian denomination viewed themselves, their Church, and the rest of the world had radically changed. Ancient rules were abolished. Women had a stronger voice in the established Church. A nun was no longer compelled to wear her habit and was encouraged to consider for herself how best she could serve her Church's mission.

◆ ◆ ◆

Confronting the crossroads in her life, Sister Anne decided to make a retreat. She explained:

> Now, a retreat is to take yourself out of your daily activities, step aside. Usually we find a sister or a priest who can speak about God and help you understand what God is talking about. Why you might be called to do a certain thing. And you listen carefully to what God is saying. You listen to your heart about what you want to do. You have this whole cycle of stuff that goes on in your head. And I thought, Oh Lord if you really want me to be a doctor, you are going to have to show me. . . . You talk this over with your spiritual director, who is a person of great faith, who can guide you in your way, to have your prayer life improved, so that you actually listen to God. Not just pray, God give me this, God give me that, but say, did I really hear you say that? Did

you really mean that? Was this a call from God, or is this just a call from John?

So anyway, the priest who was directing me was a tall guy. He was at least six foot four. He had one eye. He said, "Sister, it's very simple. The doors will open." That was it.

And the other thing was being religious. I had a vow of obedience. So I had to find out if my religious community thought this was appropriate, something they thought I should do. So I went up to Albany, New York, where our provincial house was. The community is divided up into provinces, nothing to do with the states. I went up to the provincial house and sat down with Elizabeth, who was the Superior. The Provincialist is what we called her. I said this is what's happening. I'm getting this message from my doctor that I should become a doctor, and I don't know if I want to be a doctor. I'm troubled. I don't know.

"Oh," she said, "just a minute." She opens up her desk drawer, pulls out a folder, and pulls out pictures. The pictures were of nuns in Key West in the early 1900s during the Yellow Fever epidemic. They had put on aprons . . . they were teachers and they became instant nurses there in Key West. And they had the sick people in the classrooms . . . and they took care of them . . . and they sent novitiates down from Canada who were still learning to be nuns. They sent them down to help because there were so many people who were dying. I don't know if they knew how to take care of people with such fever in those days. But anyway, some of those young women died. And in the cemetery, it's Sister Mary So and So, seventeen years of age, three hours of religious vows. They were allowed to make their vows on their deathbed.

She is showing me pictures, and I'm asking myself, Should I really go into medicine? And I realized I really should go into medicine. It was an instant decision. Yes God, you really are calling me.

For Sister Anne Brooks, "Going to medical school was a chance to show God's love on earth. . . . When I was in the waiting room [of a doctor's office] I used to see people hurting very badly, and a fair number of them were blaming God. . . . My motivation was to let them know that God does care. The practice of medicine to me is wanting to communicate God's love." Her treatment from John Upledger led her to want to become a doctor of osteopathy: "He made me realize there was more to being a doctor than just medicine." Sister Anne's habit went to the back of her closet.

Chapter Eight

ACTIVATING HER POWER

Hold fast to dreams, / For if dreams die, / Life is a broken-winged
bird / That cannot fly.
—Langston Hughes

In 1978 Sister Anne, forty years old, moved to Lansing, Michigan, to
take the required pre-med courses she needed before entering the
College of Osteopathic Medicine at Michigan State University in
East Lansing. Dr. Upledger had moved from Florida to Michigan the
previous year to become a full professor at the College of Osteopathic
Medicine. Throughout her years of pre-med and medical school, Anne
felt deeply grateful for his constant encouragement and support. Out
of her wheelchair and back brace and relatively free of debilitating
pain for the first time in eighteen years, her whole life opened up
in new, challenging, and wonderful ways. In addition to her coursework, she found employment with the medical personnel pool to
give administrative support to the visiting nurses at St. Lawrence
Hospital in Lansing. She also served as the lay minister in a vibrant
student parish and was an unofficial hospital chaplain. Additionally,
she worked with brain-damaged children in a special hospital ward.
In the summer of 1980, she was sent to Europe and spent a month in
France and a month in England studying and teaching as an assistant
professor at the École Européenne d'Ostéopathie. Her life had become
a whirlwind of activity!

In 1982, after successfully completing her coursework in the bio-
medical and clinical sciences at the College of Osteopathic Medicine
at Michigan State University, she served the following year as an
intern at Riverside Osteopathic Hospital in Trenton, Michigan. In 1983
Sister Anne received, cum laude, the degree of Doctor of Osteopathic
Medicine. Thenceforth, her official title was Sister Anne Brooks, DO.
Most folks would simply address her as Dr. Brooks.

The previous summer she had begun the search for a position
where she could fulfill her obligation to repay her full tuition schol-
arship from the National Health Service Corps (NHSC). She needed
to use her newly acquired medical skills to serve "a vulnerable and
underserved population approved by the NHSC" for three years.
Sister Anne didn't have a clue as to how she should start looking.
The NHSC published a large directory of areas that were in need
of medical services. So with this as her reference guide, she pulled
out the atlas to see where she might want to go. "Not the north, the
south is warmer."

In the summer of 1982, between her coursework and internship,
Sister Anne traveled around for a month, making inquiries, meeting
some interesting people, but she garnered no potential leads. Since
traveling about was producing no leads, she decided to write letters
and sent over forty inquiries to various places around the country
that were listed in the NHSC directory. Only one town responded—
Tutwiler, Mississippi. Sister Anne received a letter from Mayor Johnny
W. Jennings, stating, *We are interested in having you come to Tutwiler.*
Later that fall, Sister Anne met the mayor and board of aldermen in
Tutwiler for an interview. After the mayor introduced her, she rose
to her feet, thanked the mayor, and said, "I want to tell you first off,
I'm a Catholic sister and I'm a doctor. And if that's a problem, let
me know now, and I'm out of here." After a minute or two of dead
silence, one of the aldermen stood up and said, "Doctor, I want you
to know we have $19,000 of city revenue dollars to fix up the clinic."

Sister Anne was stunned! She'd had no idea they had a clinic. "My
heart began to beat really fast . . . a clinic . . . UNBELIEVABLE. . . . This

beautiful, furnished, locked-up building was just standing there in the middle of nowhere, waiting for a doctor. I'm staying in Tutwiler . . . and next they found me a house."

◆ ◆ ◆

Before moving to Tutwiler, Sister Anne wanted to know more about her new home. As was her way for approaching any new situation she did her research and learned that in its early days, Tutwiler had been a busy railroad stop town with dozens of trains coming through every day. However, in 1983, although many freight trains still rumbled through Tutwiler, none of them stopped. The depot that had been built almost ninety years before was gone. All that was left in the center of Tutwiler was the rail bed, a concrete slab, and a wall memorializing the legendary 1903 encounter between blues legend W. C. Handy and an unnamed musician.

A bit of railroad history helped Anne understand the town's economic rise and fall, plus some of the cultural lore of the Mississippi Delta. Before the final decades of the nineteenth century, the Mississippi Delta was the home to a system of short, antebellum, narrow-gauge railroad lines that formed a haphazard network throughout the region. In the 1890s those fragmentary, independent lines were consolidated, and lumber companies from the northern states and England bought up hundreds of thousands of acres of the area's ancient timberland. Giant oak, hickory, loblolly pine, and chestnut trees were cut down and hauled to dozens of sawmills that were built beside those railroad tracks. Because of the proximity of the railroads to timberlands and lumber mills, plus a climate that allowed for year-round work, more than 60 percent of Mississippi's industrial workers were lumbermen at the start of the twentieth century. The state ranked third among the nation's lumber-producing states. Almost immediately after those virgin forests were razed, the land was cleared for the planting of cotton in the region's rich alluvial soil. The railroad companies were eager to consolidate further and expand their reach in transporting the burgeoning amount of cotton being grown in the area.

As the Illinois Central Railroad extended its rails north, a new "Tutwiler" stop was identified and named for Tom Tutwiler, the civil engineer who was working on the railroad's expansion. In 1900 a depot was erected at this Tutwiler stop. The new depot was a two-story building, and the company gave the top floor to the town for use as a public school. That Tutwiler stop soon expanded into a small but lively town. As the railroads grew, so did the town, with as many as twenty-three passenger trains a day coming though and going in four different directions from Tutwiler. Still today, local residents say that W. C. Handy, the Father of the Blues, first heard the blues played by a plantation field hand sitting in the Tutwiler train station, where "the Southern cross the Dog," as the crossing tracks were called. (Other Mississippians claim that Handy was in Moorhead on that epical day.)

Tutwiler was incorporated in 1905, and its population, over 90 percent African American, grew at a steady pace to reach a little over a thousand in the 1920s. However, in 1929, during the financial crisis, the town lost its railroad center. In the following years, the increasing mechanization of both farming and the lumber industry severely diminished the town's former economic base. Unemployment eventually became rife, although the land remained a source of great riches. The soil, probably the most fertile in the nation, produced a bounty of rice, cotton, and soybeans, but the money eluded the field hands and sharecroppers who previously had worked the land. After World War II, the giant machines of the agricultural revolution replaced them and their livelihood. This brief history helped Sister Anne understand the roots of Tutwiler's current poverty.

◆ ◆ ◆

Shortly after Sister Anne moved to Tutwiler, she befriended Panny Mayfield, who introduced the new doctor to the area and also became her patient. Panny had grown up in Tutwiler in the 1930s and '40s.

In fact, she as a young girl had lived in the same house that became home to Sister Anne and the nuns when they moved to Tutwiler. Panny remembers, "Tutwiler was a busy railroad town with places like Lula Mae's Sunrise Café, located not far from the depot and within easy walking distance to Foster's Shoe Repair Shop that angled across the street from Lomenick's Meat Market." She nostalgically recalled "the Tutrovansum Movie Theatre [which had combined the first three letters of Tutwiler with the initial letters in the names of the neighboring towns of Rome, Vance, and Sumner]. The theater was the main attraction for teenagers and their tag-along younger siblings on Saturday afternoons." Now all that was all gone. The commercial, civic, recreational, community energy had disappeared. So very much had changed.

◆ ◆ ◆

In the fall of 1983, when Sister Anne Brooks became the medical director of the Tutwiler Clinic, which was located in Tallahatchie County, this county was considered to be the most impoverished place in the United States. The clinic's structure, built twenty years before in 1963, was 2,100 square feet. It contained a waiting room for white patients, a waiting room for black patients, a delivery/surgery procedure room, and two small rooms where patients could be observed in bed. An x-ray machine and a small lab, as well as two completely furnished treatment rooms, made the clinic complete, according to the guidelines for the Rural Health Initiative (RHI) project that had funded its construction. The ownership of the building and its contents had reverted to the town of Tutwiler when the project was no longer funded by the national government. Unable to retain a medical director, it had been closed and shuttered for five years.

The doctors who had come to Tutwiler before Dr. Brooks stayed only as long as they were required to fulfill their obligation to the National Health Service Corps, which had funded their medical education. No doctor wanted to stay in Tutwiler, Mississippi. And in 1977 the town had to close the clinic because no licensed doctor would come to a place so mired in poverty. Over 90 percent of the population was undereducated, with a large percentage illiterate, and the place was economically decimated. Because of the mechanization of agriculture, unskilled manual labor was no longer needed in the fields, and historic racism was still very much in evidence. Tutwiler's population was trapped in a place with little to no opportunity—a place of no hope.

But Sister Anne Brooks, DO, saw it very differently. She felt God had called her to Tutwiler, Mississippi, "the bottom of the barrel," a place where she could serve His calling. Excited by what she believed to be providential, she embraced the challenge as an answer to her prayers—a call to apply her newly earned medical knowledge, teaching experience, and compassionate heart to help an impoverished, largely segregated people.

Was it providential that Sister Anne landed in Tutwiler, Mississippi, five miles north of Sumner, Mississippi? The name Sumner was emblazoned in her memory. It was the town where the trial of the murder of Emmett Till took place in 1955. Twenty-eight years earlier, during her first few months as a postulant in the Convent of Holy Names in Rome, New York, Emmett Till's murder had been the lead story in national and international news publications. Kitty Brooks, the young postulant, had read every word she could find. It was a story that made a lasting impression on the future Sister Anne Brooks, DO. She became dedicated to fighting racism and the poverty it created.

In a comprehensive report about Tutwiler Clinic in 2000, she included a detailed, eighteen-page timeline (1954–2000) of every significant happening in the civil rights movement. [See appendix 4.] Sister Anne said, "I was deeply impressed by Mamie Till Bradley's dignity and unwavering sense of purpose in wanting to expose the cruel injustice under which her race suffered."

◆ ◆ ◆

With a $19,000 grant from the town of Tutwiler and $30,000 from Catholic Extension, SA, Dr. Brooks was able to renovate the twenty-year-old clinic. Her first priority was combining the two segregated waiting rooms—the wall between the two was removed. On August 15, 1983, when Dr. Anne Brooks, DO, officially reopened Tutwiler Clinic, there was only one waiting room. Three other sisters from her order of the Holy Names had come from Florida to serve in the clinic. Sister Josephine Louise Paleveda arrived to manage the office, Sister Zenon D'Astous was a registered nurse, and Sister Rita D'Astous (Sister Zenon's blood sister) became the lab technician, x-ray tech, and EKG tech.

The town found a two-story house, built in 1906, several blocks from the clinic for the four nuns to live together. Remarking that it was the same house where her friend Panny Mayfield had grown up, Sister Anne remembered, "It was a great home. We loved turning one room into a chapel. And when we opened the clinic, Bishop Houck came up from the Diocese of Jackson to say Mass in our living room and then went on to bless our clinic building." She later wrote, "He was quite pleased and excited about our mission."

◆ ◆ ◆

Having found her mission, Sister Anne wrote a poem.

Mississippi Delta Journey, 1983

Misty morning's gentle newness:
Sun arising, round and red
Breeze of gentle freshness teasing

MARY, NOW IS DAWN BEFORE US
Swimming rice-green paddies growing
Bristling wheat-tan acres drying
Standing scorched-black fields awaiting:

SEE THE SUN OF JUSTICE RISING
Ribbon roadways leave the Delta
Plunging quickly through the hillsides:
Kudzu ghosting stumps and forests:

JESUS, PERFECT DAY IS PRESENT
Morning breaking like creation:
Consecrated women praying—
Mississippi mission seekers . . .

SHOW US, HOLY ONE, WE'RE SEARCHING
GO BEFORE US, AS OF OLD
WE YOUR CHOSEN PEOPLE FOLLOW
TRUSTING IN YOUR SIGNS OF LOVE
HEARING NOW YOUR CALL TO HEALING
OPEN UP OUR HEARTS TO YOU

◆ ◆ ◆

Because of limited or a complete lack of previous medical care, the clinic was at first like an emergency room filled with people with incredibly serious health complications—advanced diabetes, sky-rocketing blood pressure, severe obesity, children brain-damaged by previous high fevers. Most of the patients Dr. Brooks saw were trapped in poverty and hopelessness. And too, most of her patients were black and who in 1983, according to Sister Anne, "would not trust the touch of a white person. When I first came to Tutwiler, the patients would not look me in the eye because they were black and I was white. And they knew what happened to people who looked white people in the eye. So I had to completely revise my approach to them. They didn't want to tell me '*nothin*.'"

When interviewed during her first years at the clinic, Dr. Brooks explained that "the poverty-stricken frequently have no initiative to improve themselves, because they are malnourished and are often ignorant about their own bodies. One woman brought her grand-daughter in to see me only after she had poured turpentine in the child's ear trying to ease the pain of what she thought was an ear-ache—the child actually had a ruptured eardrum." She often relied on extensive explanations to teach her patients about their bodies, recalling, "One of my patients had been hospitalized four times for an unexplained abdominal pain. He was bloated and had gas, but nothing else seemed to be wrong with him. His problem was actually very simple—he didn't know how his digestive system worked, and every time he heard his stomach rumble, he panicked—he thought he had a worm or snake inside of him. With the help of pictures, I described to him what was going on inside his body. He was absolutely flabbergasted. He's doing fine now. When people know that you're really interested in them, they begin to take a little more interest in themselves. By helping people regain their dignity and self-respect, I can help them stay in good health."

Dr. Brooks listened to her patients and met them where they were. As a matter of principle, she liked to suggest ways for patients to help themselves. Shortly after she re-opened the clinic, a man arrived with a sore back. He'd been chopping cotton in a nearby field—moving methodically up and down the rows, digging weeds with a hoe. She recommended that he spend the weekend in bed, putting hot towels on his back every few hours. Then she thought to ask if he had hot water. "No, ma'am, I don't," he told her. "But I can heat the kettle." How? She asked. "I'll go outside, haul the water and chop some wood," he said, "then start a fire." Dr. Brooks told him to rest in bed and perhaps ask a friend to rub his back.

◆ ◆ ◆

Her days were long. She got up every morning at 5:30 a.m. for an hour of private prayer, followed by group prayer at 7:00 with the other nuns at their house. At 7:30 her typical workday began with her rounds, checking on the more critically ill patients she had admitted to the nearby Regional Medical Center in Clarksdale. From 9 a.m. to 6 p.m. she saw patients at her office and frequently was called in the middle of the night for a house call to a frightened, sick individual.

With compassion and understanding and a holistic approach to medical care, Dr. Brooks gradually began to gain her patients' trust. "When I didn't leave after a year, which I gather most of the preceding doctors had done, they began to say, 'Oh she's still here, maybe I can trust her a little bit.' When I would show up at the hospital to see them when they were 'bad sick,' they couldn't believe it. You went to hospital to die, and I think they figured if I were there, maybe they wouldn't die. And then when they found me coming to their homes, when they needed home care, or they couldn't get a ride some place, that helped them trust me a little more and they began to open up."

Chapter Nine

SAINTLY MEDICINE

THE TUTWILER CLINIC PHILOSOPHY

The Staff of the Tutwiler Clinic
Affirms the dignity of each person
And her or his right to quality health care
Provided in a Christian manner.

The staff seeks to enable Clinic patients
To become knowledgeable
About their health or illness
And to participate in their own care
To their fullest potential.

Most everyone called her Dr. Brooks, but she always made it clear that she was Sister Anne Brooks, DO, who believed that "a nun's job is to facilitate change in people and help them to realize that God loves them." She never considered her calling or her profession an "either/or" choice. She lived her life and offered her services both as a physician and as a nun, who was an experienced, masterful teacher with compassion and holistic understanding.

Humane Medicine: A Journal of the Art and Science of Medicine,
published by the Canadian Medical Association, October 1991, published an interview that captures Dr. Brooks's approach to patient care:

> To be allowed into a person's centre of naked pain is a special privilege.
> To search to find the spring that will trigger the body's own ability to
> heal itself, to walk with the patient's life in my hands as recovery con-
> tinues—those are the challenges I face from patients of all ages. To see
> dignity, stripped away by welfare, restored by a caring clinic staff, to
> teach Graduate Equivalency Diploma (GED) classes after clinic hours,
> the eagerness of students my own age sparking enthusiasm in place
> of my day's fatigue, to bump over rutted roads to hold a strong hand,
> now cooling in the presence of the Angel of Death, to gently move my
> hands along muscle worked to a spasm and feel it relax, to hold the
> limp form of a child dying of malnutrition—these are facets of my life
> as a sister/doctor in the Mississippi Delta.
>
> My patients have taught me that loving compassion heals—not the
> doctor. Hope heals—not the doctor. These are among the indefinable
> things that change curing into healing. Curing is what happens when
> a disease goes away. However, illness is how sickness affects one's
> relationships with others, and illness must be healed before a person
> can return to the equilibrium of health. It is thrilling to help folks rec-
> ognize their illness, to call it by name, even when it is perhaps hard to
> pronounce aloud, like leukemia. This is the beginning of them taking
> on the task of their own healing. I have come to believe that, even
> if a patient cannot be cured, healing is still possible—a healing that
> enables one to rise above one's disability and continue a meaningful
> life. So that's my role as sister/doctor—to enable, to gently coax, to
> challenge, to love, to stand strong, to facilitate healing, to receive.

◆ ◆ ◆

Sister Anne was always fully present as she listened carefully to a
patient talk about her or his problem. She would often draw pictures,

use analogies, or tell stories to explain an illness until she was satis-
fied that her directions for treatment were understood. When there
was an emergency, she was always on call. And as a gifted writer, she
would write in her journal about the heartaches and challenges she
experienced:

WILLIE: "Oh Doctor, I ain't never had such a good 'xamination!" That
was my introduction to you, Willie, the first of many office visits, as
we tried to keep you well—as well as you could be when you "flat-out"
refused to take medicine to keep your heart from "jumpin' like a goat."
How I admired you—thin, wiry, so gentle—as I saw you carefully
walking about town with your "quad" cane, your only concession to
your age. I worried about you each time I left town, but each time, you
were there when I returned.

Then I got that call from Essie; my heart was in my throat as I hurried to your house as fast as I could through town. (That house was
unfit for human habitation, sub-standard they call it.) There you were,
lying face up on the floor by the back door. I thought for a moment
you had gone to God but, no, you were just terribly weak and scared,
and so was I. I didn't know if you had had a stroke—or maybe a heart
attack or pneumonia. So we called the "sick wagon" and got you up to
the hospital.

That was the day I saw your boss-man, and he told me what a fine
hand you were, how you never got drunk and always worked harder
than anyone else. (I wondered where your retirement benefits were,
and how come you stayed in that falling-down house . . .)

It turned out you were just dehydrated from lying there so long, but
it kind of took the "oomph" out of you. Someone was kind enough to
take you and care for you at their home. That's where I saw you last,
Willie, lying skewed across that hospital bed in the small window-
less area they called your "room." I was leaving to go out of town to a
meeting and your smile just lit up your face when you saw it was me
tickling your foot. But when I came back to town, you had gone, and I
hadn't said goodbye. I guess I didn't see the Lord standing by your bed

that day. But I know one thing—When I see you again, I 'spect to see you standing next to Him, all straight and proud.

ALBERTA: "Even if you ARE white, I'm gonna hug you!" She was in her early 60s, gnarled by years bent picking cotton. I recalled her first visit, three weeks before, when her sour look had reflected the toll of incessant pain. All I had done was examine her, diagnose degenerative joint disease and give her an anti-inflammatory pill, requesting that she return. Now she had her strong arms around me, her toothless smile lighting her weathered face. We held close in a moment of communion. Shackles of race, pain and poverty shattered. I had become HER doctor.

THE BABY IN ROME: The phone rang. Quickly I dried my hands and clipped my "beeper" to my slacks. "Hello, Dr. Brooks speaking."

"Mary Ann just radioed from the van and said there was an accident in Rome. She said a baby was hurt."

"Coming," I said, slamming the phone down. I grabbed my doctor bag and my keys, leaped down the porch steps and fumbled with the stubborn seat belt as I started the jeep. Shoving aside the blanket that covered the radio, I grabbed the mike. "Luke One to TC base."

"TC base, come in," Sister Cora Lee, my nurse, immediately answered.

"Get the emergency bags and meet me out front."

"10–4." I laid the mike on the seat.

In another minute I pulled up at the clinic, and Cora Lee hopped in, throwing the bags in the back seat. Dodging the potholes, we swung out onto the highway. No one turning at the Jitney store. . . . Road clear. Headlights. Flashers. The emergency light was in the other car. Bummer. Slung west on 49 around the curve. Pigue's house shimmered in the June sun. Farm talk chattered on the radio.

"Where in Rome did Mary Ann say the wreck was?"

"I don't know."

I thought of the tiny settlement of squalid field hands' quarters, the gas station, the two or three gravel roads, the once proud brick buildings that lined the main street.

The speedometer needle crept up. Only 3 more miles to go . . .

"Breaker! Breaker!" Cora Lee's voice had a taut edge to it. "Luke One to Outreach."

"Outreach. Go ahead."

"Where exactly are you?"

"At the turn off the highway."

Rounding the last curve we saw it. An 18-wheeler lay jackknifed several yards off the highway to the left. About 20 people were standing around. I swung onto the shoulder. "You get the driver, and I'll take the baby," I said.

A small group stood around the baby lying on the grass. A young man was kneeling beside it, pushing on its chest. He looked up as I put the bag down. "I did everything I could," he choked. I knelt beside him and ripped off the baby's bloody shirt. The child looked not even 6 months old. Briefly listening to the steady heartbeat, rapid between the pounding beats of my own heart, I suddenly realized there were no spontaneous respirations. Automatically I cleared the airway and placed my mouth over the baby's bloodied lips. Airway open, good chest motion . . .

In between breaths I ran my hand under the diaper. Lots of shards of glass, not many cuts. The baby's ear was streaming blood. "Bad sign," I thought. Puff . . . puff. . . . Heart still going well. I settled back for a long haul.

"Anyone call an ambulance?" A chorus of yeses answered me. "Yewle," I said, spotting one of my patients. "Can you get the blanket from the jeep?" His worried look eased a little as he ran to get it. Puff . . . puff. . . . We eased the blanket around the small body. Bruising was apparent now under the eyes of the baby. How long had those pupils been fixed wide? Puff . . . puff. . . . Heart still strong. . . . A siren shrilled in the distance. Puff . . . puff. . . .

Sister Cora Lee joined me. "The truck driver is stable," she said. "some bad cuts, but he wanted to know how the baby is." Some bystanders were holding a towel over us to block the sun. God bless them. Puff . . . puff. . . . "Heart is good." She nodded.

The ambulance screeched to a halt. Two nurses jumped out, gloved, holding an Ambu bag for breathing. I looked at my own hands red with dried blood. The risk of AIDS had never entered my head. Somehow it seemed part of a distant world. Puff . . . puff . . . puff . . ." Where's the pediatric mask?" the nurse screamed. Puff . . . puff . . . Cora Lee's voice sounded anxious as she held her stethoscope to the tiny chest. "Heart's slowing."

My back suddenly began aching, and I realized I'd hunkered down for awhile. They had found the mask and came to bag the baby. I knelt up straight for a moment, looking at Cora Lee's stethoscope. Her eyes met mine. "Stopped," she said. I moved my fingers to the breast bone and began pint-sized chest compressions. Someone brought the spine board, and we gently eased the floppy form of the baby onto it. I wondered if it was a boy or a girl. I wondered . . . my thoughts broke off as I heard Cora Lee. "Lift on the count of three. One, two, three." We placed the board in the ambulance, the nurses continuing their CPR. A woman suddenly appeared at my side. "Can I go?" she asked. "I'm the baby's grandmother." I directed her to the front seat, wondering if she knew the baby was probably not going to live.

"OK," the nurse yelled, and we slammed the door shut. The silence was thick in the noon sun. Tears welled up in my eyes as I heard choking sobs from the young man who had first been helping. I held him close as he bent over, vomiting. "You did all you could," I said helplessly. "That's what matters."

All we could, I thought. How hard to have that tiny life slip away under our fingers. All we could do. And yes, it mattered. Mattered a whole lot that we tried. Mattered that we cared. . . . I blinked fast and turned to help Cora check out the other passengers leaning against the front of the crumpled car.

MAN WALKER: Man died today. Man Walker, age 55, plantation field hand. Man whose boss-man recently had allowed his family to move into a brick house on the Place. Man who had kept silent from fear of eviction after a suspicious chest x-ray. Man died today, a victim, 2 months after he first came to the clinic for an unending cough, one year after that fateful test.

The jeep jerks and swerves over the rutted road as I respond to the call from his sister a few minutes earlier: "Turn off at the white fence, the one at the pecan grove." The chickens scatter indignantly as the jeep bounces over the bayou bridge, dust billowing in the air. Pulling up just short of the ditch, I run into the house, white coat flapping.

And there is Man, lying on the sofa, making small gasps like a fish out of water, eyes closed, heart pounding, sweat rolling down his handsome face. His wife stands by, stoic in her knowledge of his death.

"Go talk to him," I say. "Talk loud in his ear, and tell him how much you love him." Tears stream down our faces as she kneels beside the worn couch, taking his calloused hands in hers. Their children huddled behind her, wide-eyed and scared, touching their father for the last time, communicating all their hearts are unable to express in words. There is time to wipe his face only once before his laboured breathing ceases and his hands go limp.

"He pass?" The oldest daughter's voice is husky and soft. Stethoscope to chest, I hear the last of widely spaced heartbeats. I nod, automatically glancing at my watch. My fingers trace the sign of the cross on his forehead. His son brings a quilt to cover him. Neighbors come in silently, only to break into loud sobs when they realize they have come too late. For a moment, I hold his wife and children close and then slip out quietly, leaving them to the ministry of their friends.

Man died today.

The jeep just misses the ditch as I maneuver back to the road. The dog sits in his usual place in the sun, lazily scratching. The chickens are pecking under Georgia's house now, well out of the way. Someone has started the tractor, its loud motor shattering the silence. L.W. looks up from his repair work on the cotton picker and waves. The dust stirs in little whirlwinds as I turn onto the highway.

Man Walker, you took part of my heart with you when you passed today. May the angels lead you into paradise, and may the martyrs come to welcome you. May all the saints march with you up to the door of the Big House, and may the Lord open the door wide, and invite you in, forever.

◆ ◆ ◆

Sister Cora Lee Middleton, RN, who joined the clinic staff in 1984 a year after it opened and served with Sister Anne for over thirty years, observed that "Dr. Brooks has the ability to focus on one patient, as if he or she is the only one in the world. She is very attentive, and at the same time, she can tell patients some pretty hard stuff about their conditions."

Sister Anne's practice was built on her belief that the most important thing between a doctor and a patient was *trust*. In the years when her arthritis was cripplingly acute, many doctors had treated Sister Anne, but Dr. John Upledger was the first she truly trusted. And Dr. Upledger helped her walk without pain.

She believed his treatment had shown her, the future Dr. Brooks, the essential ingredient of healing was the patient's total trust in the doctor. She had learned that building such trust took time. It meant listening to try to understand a patient's total situation. It meant empathy so the patient understood that the doctor did care. It meant patience and clear language and pictures to make sure the patient understood his or her problem. It meant clear instructions for taking medicine and what not to eat, drink, or do. It meant honesty and hope that the patient would follow the instructions, take the medicine and become involved in the healing process.

At some point along the way, Sister Anne stopped wearing a crucifix, a cross with a figure of Jesus, which is different from a bare cross. "A lot of my friends were wearing a crucifix but I wore a naked cross—a blank cross." She had meditated about why she chose the blank cross. To Sister Anne, the image of Jesus on the cross, symbolized suffering. "I follow that cross not to suffer but to give. When you follow Jesus, his life and ongoing presence, you are giving of yourself, not suffering. It's hard to explain . . . When I wear a plain cross, a naked cross, Jesus shows umpteen possibilities of how to give to others . . . infinite possibilities . . . thousand things can show up, when you open yourself up, smiling all the time."

Chapter Ten

PHYSICIAN/MANAGER/ TEACHER/NUN

By 1983, when Dr. Brooks established her practice, Tutwiler's health-care system had virtually collapsed. Preventive care was unobtainable. Emergency care was at best a half hour away. She and her staff are heroes, they take nothing for themselves and give everything. She's made a real commitment to this community.
—The Baxter Allegiance Foundation

In January 1985, seventeen months after the clinic opened, it had seven hundred patients. Its one waiting room with twelve chairs was painfully inadequate. Most of the sick who came to be treated had to wait, standing in a hallway. In what became known as Dr. Brooks's "can-do" style, she recognized the problem and found a way to fix it. "We scrambled around and got a grant from Raskob Foundation," a family foundation that funds domestic and international projects of institutions and organizations identified with the Catholic Church. "I was the 'architect,' and the local lumber company bailed me out with my plan to add fourteen feet across the whole front of the Clinic. It worked!" Tutwiler Clinic now had an adequate reception area.

During those initial years the small clinic staff relied heavily on volunteers. Articles were placed in professional publications asking for doctors, dentists, and nurses to serve on a volunteer basis. Those who responded were carefully vetted, not only for their medical knowledge and experience, but also for a caring commitment. Locally, the need for volunteers spread by word of mouth. Those who came may have had very limited, if any, education, and no specific skills or job experience. They, too, were vetted but on different criteria—character, commitment, and an ability to learn. Dr. Brooks, an experienced and gifted teacher, enjoyed helping develop individuals from the local community.

When seeing a patient, she focused on the overall needs, as well as the specific health problems. She knew that long-term health depended on so much more than treatment of a specific disease or infection. Dr. Brooks looked for ways to care for major problems in a patient's life. She found and trained volunteers to supervise a day care program at the clinic and help her teach classes in such areas as basic child care skills, remedial reading, and birth control. Tutwiler Clinic soon became the gathering spot for the community. However, those local volunteers had been recruited for short-term placement. From the very beginning, her goal was to find individuals to train for paid positions, while raising the money for their salaries. Ultimately, she was determined not to have to rely on unpaid workers.

The first Sunday after Sister Anne arrived in Tutwiler in 1983, she had attended the closest Catholic church in the area, which was St. Elizabeth in Clarksdale. At the end of the service she got up to announce the reopening of the Tutwiler Clinic and had asked for volunteers. Betty Barbieri, a bookkeeper, was at that service and a few days later called Sister Anne to volunteer her services. In the early years, Betty said, she was called upon any time the clinic had a problem with their financial records—"Which was always." In 1989, after two bookkeepers working for the clinic had quit in less than two months, Betty told Dr. Brooks, "I'll do your books." Dr. Brooks replied, "Not unless you work for me." In 2017 Betty was still working for Dr. Brooks.

Cindy Herring, who years later also came to work at the clinic, said, "Dr. Brooks recruited most of us in an unconventional way." Cindy related that she was working in post-discharge records at the hospital in Clarksdale. One evening she was fretting to herself about the lack of challenge but feeling too old to look for another job, when she got a call from Dr. Brooks. "Cindy, can you get me the records of John Smith?"

"Do you know his date of birth?"

"No."

"His address?

"No. I think he was there sometime last October."

Cindy found the records and called back Dr. Brooks, who thanked Cindy and asked, "Do you want another challenge?"

"Sure."

"I want to offer you a job."

Stunned and elated, Cindy went to work for Dr. Brooks. She said, "It was an answer to a prayer."

◆ ◆ ◆

About three months after the clinic reopened, Sister Anne readied for the drive to Clarksdale for her early-morning hospital rounds and went to her car parked in the clinic parking lot. Before opening the car's door, she noticed something stuck on her windshield. She grabbed a flyer, read it, and threw it into the trashcan. The week before, she had hired her first black employee, and as a warning the Klan had put their newspaper under the wiper blade. For the next couple of days, she said, "I went on about what I was doing with this huge knot in my stomach. Nothing ever happened."

◆ ◆ ◆

At the end of her four-year obligation to the government to serve in an impoverished area to pay for her medical training, Sister Anne had decided that when her formal term of service was over, she would stay on in Tutwiler for the rest of her life. In December 1987 an article written by Les Lindeman, "The Healing of Soul and Body," appeared in the magazine *50 Plus*. Lindeman had traveled to Tutwiler to interview Sister Anne and described her as "wearing light, wire-rimmed glasses, a bright patchwork-quilt patterned skirt and a long white jacket. Around her neck, a small pewter cross hangs on a chain. Her features are sympathetic, and she speaks in a soft voice that—even without the local accent—captures the easygoing flavor of southern speech."

Les Lindeman's personal observations in his interview create an outstanding word picture of his meeting with Dr. Brooks and what he saw at the clinic in 1987. When he arrived in town, he saw only deteriorating desolation and no street signs. But eventually he found someone who could point him to the clinic.

The clinic is a small red building partially surrounded by tall pines. There are 22 small chairs in the waiting room, and half of them are filled. . . . Down the corridor, Sister Anne is examining a patient. There are patients in several of the 10 examining rooms, and six in the waiting area.

[. . .] Here in the Delta, doctors are 20 to 30 miles apart, and each is responsible for thousands of patients. Consequently, there are no doctors to cover for Sister Anne, and she is apt to answer calls at any hour of the day or night, every day of the year, except for the two weeks when she goes on religious retreat. She seldom travels out of beeper range—about 15 miles.

"For me, the poverty vow pertains especially to my time," she says. She fights against the urge to "hoard" her evenings and her Sunday afternoons, "but it's a hard battle." Often the battle is decided for her. Last Sunday afternoon a woman came by with a sore leg, and she took her over to the clinic. While she was there, another woman called to say that her husband had just had a stroke, and that meant a drive to the hospital. Just last night a boy in bare feet stepped on a sharp piece of tin and needed 12 stitches; another night this week, a mirror fell off a wall and cut a young boy as he was washing for dinner. "I've been doing a lot of sewing lately," she says.

That bit of dark humor is a thin defense against the great amount of sadness she faces every day. She is certain that without her built-in support system—the sisters who live and work with her—the job would be impossible.

◆ ◆ ◆

Sister Anne later remarked that with the years she had begun to mellow.

I don't panic when I see someone come in with a brown recluse spider bite that's going to eat up their face. I have delivered eighteen babies outside the hospital in adverse circumstances. The most recent was in a car in the back yard of our house. It was a twenty-one-year-old woman, seven months pregnant, who was expecting twins. This was her fifth and sixth child. There was a huge thunderstorm, and my RN clinic coordinator was out there with me handing me umbilical cord clamps, and the counselor was warming blankets in the oven in our kitchen, while the daddy and other four children looked on from the front seat. It was a very interesting experience. I didn't panic. I would have panicked early on. The mellowness that comes with age and grace and wisdom has played a part in that, also. I no longer have a heart attack when someone comes in with a heart attack.

In addition to the "mellowness that comes with age" and experience, Dr. Brooks has a certain droll, some say rascally, sense of lightheartedness. On some days you might see a little rhythmic skip in her step as she headed for her Brownie Box in her office. Her Brownie Box was a big, lidded, tin box that perhaps might better be called her "Bribe Box." When one of her staff, knowing of her special fondness for chocolate, wanted a special favor, he or she arrived in Dr. Brooks's office with a batch of freshly baked brownies before submitting the request. And, too, there were other times when the box was surreptitiously filled as an anonymous thank-you from a grateful patient or member of her staff.

Chapter Eleven

REBIRTHING A COMMUNITY

Challenges are what make life interesting, and overcoming them is
what makes life meaningful.
—Anonymous

In addition to providing medical care, the clinic was creating programs
to heal the whole person. In the mid-1980s Sister Maureen Delaney,
also a member of the Order of the Holy Names of Jesus and Mary,
was working in California as a community organizer. She heard that
Sister Anne Brooks, who ran the Tutwiler Clinic, was looking for
someone to do outreach work. Sister Maureen was deeply impressed
with Sister Anne's comprehensive approach to patient care—her focus
on treating the whole person.

Sister Anne went beyond treating only the body's illness. One
patient, who had no phone and could not read and was rearing the
child of a family member who was in jail, told Sister Anne that she
had not received her Social Security check in months. Sister Anne
took charge. She insisted that the patient come to the clinic to use
the clinic's phone and helped her track down her missing checks.
This approach resonated with Sister Maureen. She wanted to be a
part in helping treat some of the endemic ills of Tutwiler, Mississippi.

Sister Maureen contacted Sister Anne and told her, "What I do is
community organizing. I talk to people about what kind of things
they want to have happening." Dr. Brooks explained that people didn't

even have a place to gather to talk about ways to make the town better. She said, "Tutwiler at that point was pretty pitiful. People lived in shacks with no inside plumbing, and there was a whole lot of need."

Sister Maureen was hired and came to Tutwiler in 1987. She started her work in a back room of the clinic. Before talking to the people of Tutwiler, she thought that "people were going to say, 'I want housing, I want employment.' I am sure they wanted that, but the needs were very simple and basic to start with, so that was quite amazing to me. The first order of business was a town cleanup."

Genether Spurlock, who in 2009 was the first black woman to be elected mayor of Tutwiler, is currently a part-time employee at the Tutwiler Community Education Center. Spurlock has vivid memories of the stir Sister Maureen made when she first came to town. "I was at home one day, don't remember the year. I was a public school teacher in primary grades—home relaxing, and a friend of mine, Alberta Mitchell, came and knocked on the door and said, 'There's someone in town I want you to meet. She wants to do something for the town . . . wants to help.' . . . We went to meet with Sister Maureen, who came to do outreach at the clinic, and the first thing we [decided to do] was a town cleanup. I'd been here all my life, and [her dedication to organizing us] made me work harder. We planned for many days. The whole town came together. Even took the fire hose and cleaned the streets. We had a ball."

Dr. Brooks remembered, "It was fairly spectacular. There were street vendors selling their wares, a flatbed truck for the mayor to stand on to give a speech. They asked me to speak. Everyone was there. Black people, white people, everyone working alongside one another—it was breaking down barriers people didn't even recognize as barriers."

Sister Maureen got the people together again and continued to listen. "The next thing the people wanted was a Christmas parade for the town. A Christmas parade? OK. . . . that's what I had learned. You take people where they are. If that's going to bring people together, that's what I'm going to do and that's what we did and we had a great Christmas parade."

Genether Spurlock recalled, "That project brought the whole town together, black, white, all the people. Sister Maureen got people together and offered to help organize the event. A nearby town had thrown away their Christmas decorations, so Sister Maureen went and got them, and we had a great time refurbishing the bells and wreaths. We painted the big bells silver and spruced up the wreaths and put lights on them. We did a lot. And the way we got the money . . . we had bake sales and rummage sales, and dances for the children and cake walks at the fire station, . . . and the high school about six miles from here had a real good band . . . they came and we had this huge Christmas parade. That was just the highlight. Our kids got to have a parade in our town."

Realizing how much they could accomplish, they tackled other projects. Spurlock continued to recount good memories: "We made street signs, many of the streets had no signs, so we had to find a town map with the names on it. The fire chief cut big pieces of metal for us to paint the names on and the children, who could draw well and paint well, made the signs and we nailed the metal to sticks. (If Les Linderman had come to Tutwiler a couple years after he did, he could have more easily found his way to the clinic.) One little street where Mrs. Alberta Mitchell lived wasn't on the map, so we just made a sign and named it Mitchell Lane. We had prizes, and awards and a program to honor the winning teams. Everything we did, we created a celebration with food and drinks and good times."

Sister Maureen had listened to the people of Tutwiler—black and white. She encouraged them to organize and clean up their town, have a Christmas parade for their children, and erect signs for the streets of their town. Historic racial barriers began to crumble as the people of Tutwiler worked together to improve their town. Genether Spurlock reminisced in an interview in 2017, about those early days when the clinic's outreach program was established.

Tutwiler's population was more than it is now. A lot of our children have gotten grown and moved on. It's less than 2,000 now. I'd say it was about 3,000 then. A lot of people are gone. There were a lot of people in the surrounding areas, in the plantation houses and such, and they are all gone now. It was a lot of fun. . . . So we worked together. We even gave ourself a name and called ourselves the Tutwiler Improvement Association. That was the best we could do. We did that for several years, and Sister Maureen Delaney was always there, pushing and urging, and coming up with ideas, but she would always let us do the work. I always say she empowered us with a desire to do something for ourselves. I always give her credit, because everything was always right there all the time, but she showed us how to tap in. We just weren't motivated enough to do it on our own. She got the ball rolling, while we always thought we couldn't do anything. But we found out we could work together and we could accomplish something. We could make the town better. Also got the plantation people to come in and help.

◆ ◆ ◆

In just four years, against the monumental odds in such an economically depressed area, the power of Dr. Brooks's visionary leadership and "can-do" spirit had turned the clinic into a modest hub of social services. Dorothy Dodd, one of the Tutwiler natives recruited by Dr. Brooks, assisted Sister Maureen with the community organization initiatives. These included private reading lessons, an emergency food bank, distribution of donated clothing, grocery store carpool, home repair clinics, nutrition education, exercise classes, and parenting training.

"The outreach programs were a dream ever since we started," Dr. Brooks said. "You cannot correct problems by putting Band-Aids on them. Education is the only way of changing things. I like to think the kind of care we give is not just come-in-and-get-your-insulin-and-go-out. I like to think that one of the things we do is to try to restore self-respect, to inform people about their illness—which gives them some control over it. And we don't just say, "Oh, this poor person can't read.' We say, 'Hey, do you want to learn how to read? Somebody is willing to teach you.' We're trying to provide an environment for growth."

Mary Ann Willis, who did not have a high school education and whose children had no safe place to play when she began to work at the clinic in 1987, saw the afterschool program at the clinic as a "godsend" for her children. "Tutwiler was just about like a dead town, especially for the children." At that time most families in Tutwiler were fatherless, and many still are. When a mother goes to work, the children are left on their own with no supervision, no discipline after school. If a child in school gets sick, a working mother who goes home to take care of her child might lose her job. The nursery and afterschool programs at the clinic were a godsend for mothers and solved a huge problem in the community.

◆　◆　◆

In 1988 Sister Anne recruited Sister Joann Blomme, a licensed professional counselor, to join the clinic's staff to run the outreach program designed to prevent sexual abuse of children. Sister Joann also provided crisis intervention and ordinary counseling services. Two nights a week, the sisters conducted courses that high school dropouts could use to obtain their general equivalency diplomas, and when there were cuts in the funding for the federal Head Start Program, the clinic started a day care program for two- to four-year-olds. They also had a "death and dying" group, which helped family members whose loved ones had died.

Dr. Brooks's holistic approach always reached far beyond the clinic's walls. She was determined to find a solution to every problem she encountered, and when she heard that some of her patients were caught in a Catch 22 situation, she became involved. After most of the farming in the Delta became mechanized, and the field hands and sharecroppers lost their source of income, many of the landowners gave their previous workers the shacks where they and their families lived. These families thus became homeowners—but they were caught in an unsolvable predicament. There was a government program that loaned homeowners money for home repairs; however, these families did not qualify for any type of loan, since they had no jobs. They had no source of income to repay a loan.

Sister Anne knew better than to try to fight a government regulation. She went to the local United Parcel Service office, visited with the manager, and explained the families' situation, and her message was relayed to the philanthropic arm of that corporation. Families around Tutwiler received funds from UPS to pay for the needed repairs to their houses.

Always concerned about adequate housing for Tutwiler residents, Sister Anne worked closely with the board of the Delta Habitat for Humanity. Board member Frank Mitchener, a planter from Sumner and staunch supporter of Anne Brooks and of the clinic's mission, donated land next to the clinic. On that land Habitat houses with indoor plumbing, water, and sewer lines were eventually built for low-income families. Shortly after Sister Maureen Delaney arrived in Tutwiler, she joined the Habitat housing board and served as its chairman for over ten years, adding her strength to Sister Anne's concern for housing for Tutwiler residents.

Chapter Twelve

SPEAK UP AND SPEAK OUT

Next to doing the right thing, the most important thing is to let people
know you are doing the right thing.
—John D. Rockefeller

It did not take long for word to spread among the locals about the
phenomenal dedication and amazing service of Anne Brooks and the
group of nuns at Tutwiler Clinic. Articles and feature stories about
their accomplishments began to appear in newspapers from nearby
towns in the area—the Clarksdale *Press Register*, Jackson's *Clarion
Ledger*, and the Memphis *Commercial Appeal*—as well as national
publications of organizations with which Sister Anne Brooks, DO,
had an affiliation—Catholic and osteopathic organizations, and the
Michigan State alumni news. Her dedication and accomplishments
and the crying needs of Tutwiler began to speak to the hearts and
activate the consciences of many readers across the nation.

Then, on March 23, 1987, a little over four years after Dr. Brooks
had reopened Tutwiler Clinic, *People*—the national weekly magazine
of celebrities and human interest stories, with the largest readership
of an American magazine—featured an article entitled "Sister Anne
Brooks, Doctor and Nun, Practices without Preaching to the Poor."
An excerpt from that article captures her story from the perspective
of the 1980s.

The clinic has no fixed budget. It just runs, mostly on donations and whatever patients can pay, which isn't much. Some patients pay with catfish and collard greens. Lillie Mae pays for her care by peeling the labels off prescription bottles so they can be reused. Lue Bertha left a note stuck to the door: "I am going to pay. I just ain't had no money but I a show going to pay your because if it was not for your I would be dead today."

.... Sister Anne soon discovered other problems: Women don't drink water before going out in the fields to chop cotton, because there is no place to go to the bathroom and they're embarrassed, so they become dehydrated; some diabetes patients can't refrigerate their insulin because they have no electricity; and some patients have no tablespoons with which to measure medicine. "You see things here you see nowhere else. I guess we're doing a lot down here, but nothing ever seems to change. Maybe I've saved a few people from having their legs cut off from the effects of diabetes. The system crushes these people, and they are good and decent people. You can't help crying sometimes." When that happens, Sister Brooks says she cries herself to sleep while listening to Mozart, on a bed that is a board with a mattress balanced between cinder blocks. "It's funny," she says, "I don't pray for specific stuff anymore. The list is too long. I'd give the Lord too much work. My plea is that the Lord will just take care of us all."

◆ ◆ ◆

Sister Anne's soft-spoken yet impressively dynamic voice was powerful—the clinic's national donor base was growing, and she was tremendously thankful for any publicity the clinic received. But there was so much need. There was so much more she dreamed of doing. In addition to serving the clinic's current needs, she fervently wanted to reach more people by creating a national platform beyond her church and medical affiliations.

Here again, one wonders if providence was smiling down on Sister Anne when one morning, about two years after the article in

People magazine was published, Josh Howard, a producer for the *60 Minutes* television broadcast, had a dental appointment in New York City, where he lived. While sitting in the dentist's waiting room, Howard picked up the March 23, 1987, issue of *People* and, thumbing through, stopped to read the feature on Sister Anne Brooks. Nodding to the receptionist, Howard indicated he wanted to tear out the article, and she gave a thumbs-up. He tore out the four pages, folded them in half, and slipped them into his pocket. Sister Anne Brooks, DO, needed further investigation. Her story was a possibility for a program segment on *60 Minutes.*

Howard said when he first went to Tutwiler to meet Anne Brooks and see the town, "I never had met anyone like her. She exudes caring and kindness . . . and a complete helpfulness . . . she was someone I could immediately relate to. I could see how her patients would so easily relate to her. The fact that she could come into Tutwiler, Mississippi, and so thoroughly understand the problems of the people, not just their health problems, but their way of life that was contributing to their health problems is remarkable . . . she so completely related . . ."

The *60 Minutes* broadcast, produced by Josh Howard and narrated by Harry Reasoner, which aired in September of 1990 (and can still be viewed on the Tutwiler Clinic website), showed the nation in candid, undoctored footage the heroic spirit, goodwill, dedication, and commitment of Dr. Brooks and the other nuns at the Tutwiler Clinic. They were not only treating the health problems of the patients but, in a holistic fashion, addressing the crying needs and tragic conditions in the larger Tutwiler, Mississippi, community.

And the nation responded. Dr. Brooks said, "The whole *60 Minutes* experience left me speechless." During the first months after the program aired, the clinic received more than six thousand letters, countless phone calls, and packages containing everything from powdered laundry detergent to insulin; the show eventually generated twenty-one thousand donors and many new friends for Dr. Brooks and the Tutwiler Clinic.

In an interview over twenty years later, Josh Howard said that although he and Anne Brooks were from such very different backgrounds, he was so taken by her supportive, caring presence, the two of them stayed in touch with occasional visits through the years.

One time she was passing through New York, so I went out to the airport, and we had coffee for about three hours while she waited for her next flight. I just don't know anyone like her. She is so modest and self-effacing . . . she has a very gentle way, though decidedly supportive, always encouraging. . . . Very soft-spoken, low key . . . yet firm and focused and so very effective in getting things done.

Perhaps Anne's first impression is a bit deceptive. She is so soft spoken and gentle, and in meeting a nun, who has taken the vows of poverty, one might think she knew little about money. But she was no pushover. She had a very practical way of handling any job. When you see what she accomplished, you realize she was a very talented financial manager, an extremely keen administrator, and a master at raising money, as well as a gifted physician with an incredibly huge heart.

She may not have found the cure for cancer, but she cured so many people in so many ways. With her holistic approach to medicine, she [envisioned] and created the whole infrastructure for the community of Tutwiler. She saved an uncounted number of lives. . . . An uncounted number of people have earned their GEDs. An uncounted number have benefited from the Community Center. . . . She has made thousands of lives better.

Chapter Thirteen

THE REALIZATION OF A DREAM

Tutwiler was a dream come true for Sister Anne Brooks, DO.
—Marcie Biddleman, director, St. Petersburg Free Clinic

By January 1992 Dr. Anne Brooks's dream was materializing. The Tutwiler Clinic, under her direction, had been in operation for a little over nine years. It had a staff of twenty-five, and the clinic was seeing an average of 630 patients per month—25 percent of the patients were pediatric, and about 25 percent were elderly. Some of her patients were wealthy landowners and professionals in the area, but about 52 percent of the clinic's patients had no means to pay for their care. That year Dr. Brooks received the Humanitarian Award from the national Auxiliary to the American Osteopathic Association (AAOA). The Humanitarian Award is designed to honor a woman who has made an outstanding contribution to her field. That same year, Dr. Brooks also received the first Norman Vincent Peale Award for Positive Thinking.

Sister Anne Brooks, DO, was increasingly being summoned to travel out of Tutwiler, Mississippi, to receive an award or make a speech in a metropolitan city. Panny Mayfield remembers a phone call she received sometime in the early 1990s. "Panny," said Dr. Brooks, "do you think you and your mother could come over and help me decide what to wear for my talk in San Francisco next week? I'm completely at a loss." Dr. Brooks was rarely at a loss. But she knew when she needed help. Having given no thought to what she wore for almost thirty years, she never gave women's fashion a thought. As a nun it was her habit, and as a doctor in the clinic and hospital it was her white coat. She thought she should look professional before an audience of community leaders and businesspeople. (Nearly twenty years later, neither Panny nor Anne remembers what she wore for her speech in San Francisco.) In the coming years, Sister Anne was probably very relieved to learn she would wear an academic gown when giving a graduation speech and receiving one of her many honorary degrees.

◆ ◆ ◆

During the previous 1991 fiscal year, the medical services that the clinic provided had grown to be worth $402,000, for which it received $166,000 in payment. The difference was made up through donations. With all the publicity Dr. Brooks's work received in magazines and newspapers, plus the *60 Minutes* segment, which aired twice on CBS, "the money just sort of fell in my lap," she said. "Viewers sent cash and other donations, such as clothing. The clothing was then sold for ten cents to a few dollars apiece in a store [called the Bargain Barn] that is part of the clinic's outreach." Physicians across the nation were donating their medicine samples, which the clinic dispensed to patients who could not pay for prescriptions. To sustain the clinic's fundraising effort, Sister Anne began to write and publish a newsletter three times a year, which was printed, folded and stapled by inmates at a nearby prison. She laughingly recalled, "The fall issue was late because there were some escapes and a lockdown at the prison."

◆ ◆ ◆

John Vogel, director of purchasing at the Reading Hospital and Medical Center in Reading, Pennsylvania, was one of the many viewers who watched the CBS *60 Minutes* profile of Sister Anne Brooks that late Sunday in September. Vogel was a conscientious man who had become frustrated by the reports he was hearing about supplies donated to third world countries that ended up rotting in warehouses. The segment on Dr. Brooks made him realize that there were a lot of places in the United States that needed help. He also concluded that in a US-based program, it would be easier to guarantee that the donated items would reach the groups they were supposed to go to.

In early October 1990, Vogel called the Tutwiler Clinic to express his interest in trying to help, explaining to Dr. Brooks that through his business contacts and purchasing knowhow he might be able get some needed medical supplies. She could not have been more enthusiastic about his offer. Vogel called on his fellow members of the Northeastern Pennsylvania Chapter of the American Society for Hospital Materials Management. At the November meeting of the society's executive committee, he requested a $1,000 donation for the Tutwiler Clinic. It was approved and sent immediately.

At the same meeting, Vogel asked members to return to their respective hospitals and search their facilities for surplus supplies and unused equipment to send to the clinic. Response was slow in November and December, but after the turn of the new year, offerings started to pour in. Donations included laser surgery equipment, surgical instruments, wheelchairs, cribs, linens, office supplies, furniture, latex gloves, IV sets, catheters, commode chairs, walkers, infant car seats, and many other items.

Almost like clockwork, HCSC, a group purchasing organization in Allentown, Pennsylvania, offered warehouse space and the use of its trucks to haul the donations from the hospitals to the warehouse. Soon after, the owner of KS Processing, a red-bag (biohazardous) trash hauler, volunteered a forty-five-foot tractor-trailer and two drivers to make the trip to Mississippi.

On Tuesday morning, February 26, 1991, two vehicles—a car holding John Vogel and his son Steven, and the tractor-trailer stuffed to capacity—left KS Processing's office in Marcus Hook, Pennsylvania, bound for Tutwiler, Mississippi. Making only one stop to rest at

Vogel's daughter's home in Nashville, John and Steven Vogel arrived in Tutwiler on Wednesday, February 28, at eight o'clock in the morning. The tractor-trailer arrived soon after. Supplies were divided among three sites—the Tutwiler Clinic, the Clarksdale hospital, and the Bargain Barn, the local Goodwill-type store the clinic had started. By 2:00 that afternoon the truck had been unloaded and was on its way back to Pennsylvania.

Busy attending her patients in the nearby Clarksdale hospital and making a house call to a critically ill woman out in the country, Dr. Brooks was not present during most of the unloading. However, she got back in time to take the Vogels on a tour of the clinic and thank them profusely. She said, "It's wonderful that people believe in what we're doing here. The aid given by the thirteen eastern Pennsylvania hospitals and businesses that participated in John's relief effort was by far the most intricately coordinated expression of support the clinic has received. You can't place a price tag on all the donations, because you can't measure the concern and care contained in the boxes. . . . That support lets our patients know that people care, and that helps the healing process."

◆ ◆ ◆

By 1989, the clinic's outreach program that Sister Maureen started in 1987 as an essential part of Dr. Brooks's vision of holistic health had mushroomed. Because of the many activities and the growing number of people who wanted to participate, the space in the back of the clinic building very quickly became too small, and it was decided that a spin-off project from the Tutwiler Clinic should be formed. In December of 1989, the Tutwiler Community Education Center (TCEC) was officially incorporated as a nonprofit 501c(3) organization. The elected board of citizens, inspired by Sister Maureen, went to work. Nine months later, in September of 1990, with a generous grant from the Kellogg Foundation and the clinic's growing number of donors, enough money was raised to buy and rehab an old abandoned building in downtown Tutwiler, a block away from the clinic. In June of 1992 the outreach part of the Tutwiler Clinic officially moved into the ten-thousand-square-foot, renovated building that became known as the Tutwiler Community Education Center. The completed center had administrative offices, a small kitchen, a community room, a computer lab, a music room, fitness equipment, and a gym. The community center organized to operate as a separate organization from the clinic created the following mission statement:

> The Tutwiler Community Education Center, a body of local community people of all races, occupations and ages, is dedicated to the growth and development of the community of Tutwiler and surrounding areas by developing programs and events in response to the ideals, dreams and ideas of the members of the community so that each person may be filled with pride and hope for themselves and for their community.

In the ensuing years, in addition to the activities at the center, TCEC and the citizens of Tutwiler worked together on a number of civic projects. Sister Maureen, her staff, and volunteers took on project after project to improve "livability and enjoyment" in their town. With obvious pride Genether Spurlock, a longtime volunteer and eventually an employee at the center, stated, "There is a saying about teaching a man how to fish. Sister Maureen and Dr. Brooks taught us how to fish. They taught us to do things for ourselves. This center has always kept the needs of the people out front."

Lucinda Berryhill, who began working for the center the year it opened its doors, still drives a van to bring people to medical appointments and recruits people to come to the center for projects. "I would go find them, and they appreciated that." She added, "I appreciate the fact that children who come to the center get more than just a safe place to play. They come to get education; they learn morals and values here."

◆ ◆ ◆

Through the years the programs at the center evolved as needs and wants changed. In recent years, around two dozen children, aged seven to twelve, attend an afterschool program at the center. On arrival they get a snack, spend some time in the computer lab, participate in a group discussion on good choices and behavior, led by a member of the staff, and play in the gym until it is time to go home.

One of the most cohesive forces in Tallahatchie County is the music the locals play, so naturally music is the focus of another program for the children. One musician who teaches blues at the center remarked, "The kids got so good, they formed their own band and were invited to play at the opening of the Ground Zero Blues Club in Clarksdale and at the rededication of the courthouse in Sumner to honor the memory of Emmett Till."

The center became a place where other musicians honored Tutwiler's and the Delta's rich music heritage. In 2010 a famous harmonica player from California, Jon Gindick, founded the Sonny Boy Williamson Legacy Music Education and Performance Program of Tutwiler for the center. Sonny Boy Williamson II (1914–1948) is buried just outside of town. He was an American blues harmonica player, singer, songwriter, and native of Tutwiler, who was often regarded as the pioneer of the "blues harp" as a solo instrument.

Physical fitness and recreation is another major activity at the center. Teenagers come twice a week in the evenings to use the fitness equipment and to learn life skills. Seven to ten of those teens, ages sixteen to nineteen, get hired as Teen Helpers to assist in the center's afterschool care and summer programs, to receive job training from the center's staff, and to serve as role models for their young counterparts. Kayla Reynolds as a junior in high school was enthusiastic about her experience. "My work as a Teen Helper helped me mature and learn responsibility. I want to be a social worker and help children when I grow up."

The center's programs are focused not only on the youth. A group of seniors meets there to share meals and take trips together. During election years candidates hold forums at the center so citizens can ask them questions about their views on various issues. The center sponsors sports leagues and tournaments for kids and adults alike.

◆ ◆ ◆

A program that began even before the center became a separate entity from the clinic has become one of its most outstanding and long-lasting projects. The "quilters" started with one conversation when Mary Sue Robertson invited Sister Maureen to see the quilt tops she made in her home. "Mary Sue lived in a humble shack in the back of somebody's property that she used to work for. Inside she had piles of quilt tops," said Sister Maureen. The elderly woman offered that she would sell her work if someone wanted to buy it. Impressed with the neat stitches and colorful designs, Sister Maureen wondered if Mary Sue's hobby could become a cottage industry. Sister Maureen and fellow workers Mary Ann Willis and Sister Joanne Blomme found more than two dozen quilters in the area.

The art of quilt making had been passed down from generation to generation, and most of these quilters had learned how to quilt from their mothers or grandmothers. A business was born. This quilt program not only preserved the rich quilt-making tradition of these African American women; it was a way for women in the area to support themselves and their families. Mary Ann Willis emphasized, "From the beginning we wanted to help these ladies make money and also preserve the quilting tradition of the area. We started by saying they would get 80 percent of the price, and 20 percent would go into the program." The original quilters used scrap fabric, including old clothing. In more recent times they also use new fabric to make placemats, tote bags, cell phone cases, and oven mitts. They still keep 80 percent of the profit. As articles about the Tutwiler quilts appeared in the clinic's quarterly newsletter, orders from across the nation began to mount.

As the program grew, fewer women were learning the craft from their mothers, so the center started a class for those who wanted to learn. At present Mary Ann Willis is still involved in the quilting program, checking the quilters' work, handling the books, and traveling across the country to sell the products. "I love to go and sell their work, because I know the more I sell, the more they can work. This might be their income. They depend on it to pay their bills." The program has also expanded Mary Ann Willis's horizons. "I would never have gotten to travel had Sister Maureen not offered me the opportunity. I've been to some beautiful places." And when the Smithsonian Institution included quilts from Tutwiler's Community Center's quilters in the National Quilt Collection, their place in history was established.

Chapter Fourteen

IMPLEMENTING HOPE
AND HEALTH

It is not my responsibility to change the system. My job is to make a
ruckus . . . but change sure doesn't come quickly in Mississippi.
—Sister Anne Brooks, DO

When Sister Anne and the Tutwiler Clinic were featured on ABC's
Good Morning America in 1986, the footage shown contained shots of
some shacks her patients lived in. One of the landlords, a plantation
owner, became angry at the TV exposure, and tore down five shacks,
evicting the tenants. After that, Sister Anne said, "The people see a
stranger coming with a camera and feel like their homes are in danger."

She continued, "In 1991 we had an incident in which a white man
sold a [dilapidated] building in town to a black man. The white funeral
director didn't appreciate a black man fixing up a building near his
funeral home. After the black man's building was burned down, a
white plantation owner paid the black man off so there would not
be any investigation or trouble. White folks seeking to maintain the
status quo sometimes used subterfuge to hide their dedication to a
segregated society."

During Anne's time as the clinic's medical director, three-quarters
of the population of Tutwiler and Tallahatchie County was black, and
she commented on how racism remained one of the major roots of
local problems. "Many of the white people want things to look nice,

but they forget the shack at the end of their property. I expose and embarrass them sometimes, but as a doctor I'm also available to them [black and white] at all hours." Approximately 20 percent of Dr. Brooks's patient load was white. A physician by profession, she was dedicated to serving the needs of anyone who sought her medical advice—the poor and the wealthy regardless of the color of their skin.

◆ ◆ ◆

At times dealing with government agencies created another kind of problem for Sister Anne. When some of the lady quilters at the Community Center became established selling their quilts, and earning enough money to pay for much-needed home improvements and medical care, they became ensnared in a classic no-win governmental conundrum. The Internal Revenue Service discovered their incomes were high enough to be taxed and said they would lose their food stamps if they did not pay their back taxes.

This was a major frustration that Sister Anne knew was going to take some deep thinking and a whole lot of time and many contacts to find a way to fix. It was just one more challenge to add to her ongoing daily frustration. Of great concern were the deeply ingrained eating habits of her patients. "We have a major nutrition problem left over from the slave days. The diet of intestines, brains, hooves and jowl of the pig along with greens from the garden and corn bread, has persisted." Decrying the lack of adequate funding, she said, "It's hard to change when food stamps only cover seventy-eight cents per person per meal. It results in obesity, hypertension, and diabetes. The remarkable thing is that many of these people continue to walk around." Shaking her head, Dr. Brooks continued, "I saw a child not long ago, who I think is sixteen years old. I hadn't seen her since she was six months old. Now she is 267 pounds, and she sits at home all day." Then Dr. Brooks added, "And there is just such an incredible lack of knowledge or understanding of what constitutes good, basic bodily care." These people do not know how to take care of themselves.

She went on to recount other frustrating challenges she met daily. "One year, a few nights before Christmas, a fifteen-year-old who was five months pregnant knocked on my door at 2:00 a.m. to say, 'I'm having my baby.'"

"How do you know?" Sister Anne asked her. The girl said, "The feet are coming out."

"It's what you call a double footling breech," said Sister Anne. "The fetus was very dead. Her family had no car, so I drove her to the hospital."

Two nights later, a call came in around midnight from the family of an eighty-two-year-old-man with kidney failure. Again, Sister Anne drove to the hospital. The night after that, two nights before Christmas, Sister Anne was awakened by a "thunking" on her back porch. "It was a boy with a girl in his arms. He had seen a pickup truck skid off the road. There were four drunken teens in it. We had Mississippi mud up the wazoo in our house that night," but the girl survived.

◆ ◆ ◆

Sister Anne's words often spoke of the deep connection she felt with her patients. "We are all children of God. . . . There is no way you can be in the business that I am in and not be touched by the faith of patients . . . and that is the gift I receive daily. . . . The people are dignified poor, which means that they often don't have enough to eat. But they don't hurt each other over it. . . . These are the people who are forgotten. They don't need pity. They need food and doctoring and a way to hope."

These were black people of Tallahatchie County, where in 1955, over forty years before, Emmett Till was brutally murdered. Dr. Brooks was seventeen years old at the time, living over a thousand miles away, but the story seared her heart and helped to set her life course. Now living in the very county where racism had destroyed that young life, she was dedicated to doing all in her power to destroy the malefic forces that took Emmett Till's life.

◆ ◆ ◆

Sister Anne seized the opportunity to expand her outreach when
Gonzaga University, a private Jesuit university in Spokane, Washington, asked her to deliver the commencement address to their class
of 1993. Using her many voices—as a woman, a nun, an educator, a
citizen, a doctor, and a "ruckus" maker—she took this opportunity to
speak out about some of the glaring inequities of the situation and
systems in her work in Mississippi. She spoke of the indispensable
value of education and a community of caring others, while stress-
ing the individual's responsibility "to go out in the world and make
a difference. The following excerpts from her talk to the graduates
demonstrate the power of her voice:

> I know you've been counting the days and the hours! But there's some-
> thing you may have forgotten in all the excitement: YOU'VE GOT
> ONE MORE FINAL EXAM TO TAKE! And I'd like to share with you
> how to prepare for it:
>   This final is in the course entitled "My Life and How I Lived It."
> The date of your exam is anytime. The last question is asked at your
> death. And I'll even tell you the question: WHAT DID YOU DO FOR
> THESE, THE LEAST OF MY SISTERS AND BROTHERS?
>   Here's the course content: Life is a gift. . . . Right now, you are at a
> place in your lives where you have received, and received, and received
> and maybe given a little here and there. Now you are in a position of
> being able to give. . . . The reason you are alive today is to make a dif-
> ference in the lives of others.
>   To respond to the needs of people, to stand in solidarity with the
> poor, to constantly be on the lookout for ways to help people better
> themselves—that is making a difference. But to empower others is to
> make systemic change. . . .
>   Look around you—who is hurting? Who can't read? Who can't see?
> Who is too old to drive to the store? Who is unable to think clearly? If
> you search with the eyes of love, you'll always find someone to help. If

you listen with a loving ear, you will hear the voice of God. . . . [In Tallahatchie County] We have a seasonal job of chopping cotton where people are paid $23/day. They have to pay dollars to the truck driver who carries them out to the field; they are allowed to drink when they get to the end of the row, and there is nowhere for them to go to the bathroom. Is this an injustice? Does it need to be fixed? You bet!. . .

You and I both know that everywhere in our country there is need for empowerment, need for systemic change. Get out there and look around and jump in. . . . You may say. "Well, how will I know I'm on the right track? How will I know if I'm succeeding? How will I know if I'm ready for my final exam?" The answer is often only in your heart, only in the personal satisfaction that you feel. Most of the time, if you are the loving, caring hands and voice of Jesus, nobody pats you on the back (or if they do, it's in preparation for crucifixion because they feel guilty *they're* not doing it too).

But once in awhile, the answer will come to you like it did to me a few years ago: One of my elderly patients came hobbling over to the clinic. She didn't want a doctor visit, she just wanted to tell me something. So, I listened. And she said, "Now that you ladies have come, now I have a reason to get up in the morning." That was the ultimate compliment: A reason to get up in the morning . . .

◆ ◆ ◆

Following her own counsel, Dr. Anne's voice was persistent and clear in speaking out to activate others. One such effort, in an article written by Jeff Piselli in the November 1999 *Delta Business Journal*, reported on her leadership and her inspiring others. "A dedicated group of healers in this area is battling the problem of delivering quality health care to the poor, undereducated, and traditionally underserved residents of the Mississippi Delta. Members of that group met recently at a meeting sponsored by Delta New World Health Initiative at the Tutwiler Community Education Center to come up with new strategies to maintain the momentum gained during the past 30 years in welfare reform and decreasing levels of medical insurance for the Delta's poor. Part of the caregivers' challenge was to coordinate with state leaders to make certain that adequate funds were available for healthcare reform."

Dr. Brooks, who several years before had twice testified before the US House of Representatives Select Committee on Hunger and Infant Mortality, continued to use her signature style for addressing any problem. She had gathered a great deal of information on government funding for healthcare and said to those at this meeting of the Delta New World Health Initiative, "The idea is just to, at a grass roots level, get people concerned and organized to the point where we can make a change. And some of that change is simply *yelling at legislators*. There are issues that we're not really aware of. For example, there's a lot of federal money is given back to Washington, DC, if it's not nailed down in a hurry. I'm very concerned about that. . . . Some help is coming from the Mississippi State Legislature . . . but more is needed to address the problems." More pressure needs to be put on our elected representatives. At the conclusion of her remarks, Sister Anne publicly acknowledged that the clinic was making a difference in the lives of people in the Tutwiler area, but at times, "it was like trying to thaw an iceberg in a freezing arctic ocean."

Chapter Fifteen

GROWTH, CHALLENGE, AND RECHARGING

The power of one man or one woman doing the right thing for the right reason, and at the right time, is the greatest influence in our society.
—Jack Kemp

What was the power within Sister Anne's character that ignited the lights, one by one, in Tallahatchie County in the 1980s and created such a large glow that by the 1990s she was attracting a huge outpouring of national support and acclaim for her work in Tutwiler, Mississippi? Sister Anne Brooks, DO, is a highly intelligent woman of deep compassion for the poor and needy, but there is something more. There is uniqueness to her intellect. When confronted with a problem, she seeks to apprehend a situation in its entirety. To gain insight she digs deep and considers all factors in order to discover a problem's root cause before seeking the solution. The *New Oxford American Dictionary* defines *insight* as the capacity to gain an accurate and deep intuitive understanding of a person, thing, or situation. Does not Sister Anne's power rest in the combination of her deep faith, keen intellect, discerning insight, holistic understanding, and unwavering commitment to the empowerment of others?

◆ ◆ ◆

When we look at her life, we see that Sister Anne's unique power broke two glass ceilings—one of patriarchy and the other of allopathic medicine. In 1983, when she reopened the medical clinic in Tutwiler, she became a staff physician at the only hospital for the area—the Northwest Mississippi Regional Medical Center in Clarksdale. In 2000, seventeen years later, in recognition of the power of her leadership and medical skills, Dr. Anne Brooks, DO, was elected to be the chief of staff of that hospital in Clarksdale. She was the first woman and the first doctor of osteopathy to serve in that position. Her selection may have been surprising to some, because in 1983 most traditional allopathically trained doctors were highly suspicious of osteopathic medicine. In spite of the fact that she was a woman and a doctor of osteopathy, her dedication to "going the extra mile" and the response of her patients were recognized and honored by her peers.

Sister Anne would always go the extra mile. Using her emotional and physical powers, she developed incredible stamina as she overcame her physical disabilities. During her first year in Tutwiler, in addition to reopening the clinic and building its clientele, she drew on her educational experience and love of teaching to be a clinical instructor for nurse practitioner and physician assistant students from various universities in Mississippi, Tennessee, and Arkansas. Three years later she became a clinical adjunct faculty and a Mississippi preceptor for medical students from colleges of osteopathic and allopathic medicine in the United States and Toronto, Canada. Under her direction Tutwiler Clinic became a challenging residency for the professional development of both future physicians and nurse practitioners.

But the power of her teaching ability was not limited to hospital, clinic, and classroom sites. From that first year in Tutwiler, Dr. Brooks was a frequent guest speaker at the Webb/Sumner Rotary Club and the West Tallahatchie School District parent-teacher meetings and was invited to speak out of state at national osteopathic meetings. As she spread her words, her reputation grew, and she was called to give testimony on social/medical matters to various governmental bodies, both local and national. By 1995, until her retirement in 2017, she had become in many ways a media celebrity, giving more than a dozen talks a year, sometimes a dozen in one month—across the country as well as in the Mid-South area. Her overwhelming list of speaking engagements included professional conferences, civic clubs, civil rights groups, justice colloquiums, health and community-building workshops, foundation board meetings, religious societies, high school assemblies, university seminars, teacher and faculty meetings, Habitat assemblies, legislative hearings, medical meetings, community health services groups, and university extension programs. During those years she was also giving television, newspaper, and magazine interviews wherever and whenever she spoke. This remarkable woman felt compelled to tell and enjoyed the telling of the Tutwiler story. She felt a deep, personal responsibility to champion and explain the holistic–osteopathic approach to health care and community care. And she found joy in being with the hundreds of individuals she met from all walks of life. When one looks at the impressive number of honors and awards Sister Anne received over the years, it is obvious that many, many people across our nation found joy in hearing the power of her story, marveled at her dedication and accomplishments, and felt called to support her good works. And undergirding this impressive national prominence was her power as an inspired administrator with keen organizational and communication skills, and outstanding fundraising capabilities.

◆ ◆ ◆

As a physician, Dr. Brooks, this down-to-earth yet saintly nun lived by but never preached her faith to her patients. She was a compassionate, extremely effective medical doctor, who fervently believed and often stated that "the psyche, the soul, and the body are part of every human being. Each is seriously affected when a person is ill. To address each level of being is critical if the healing process is to be successful. If we do not involve our patients in our plan of care, they go away only partially better."

She was a physician who was very serious about involving patients in their own care. Cindy Herring, Dr. Brooks's administrative assistant, recounts that many times she overheard Dr. Brooks in firm, no-nonsense straight talk say, "Now, [patient's name], you have to take your medicine. *If you don't take your medicine as prescribed, you are going to die.*"

As a highly respected professional, she was a fellow of the American College of Osteopathic Family Physicians and was honored by her peers when she was asked to deliver the annual Andrew Taylor Still Memorial Address to the House of Delegates of the American Osteopathic Association (AOA) meeting in Chicago, Illinois, on July 17, 1993. Andrew Taylor Still (1828–1917) was the founder of osteopathy and osteopathic medicine. In her remarks, 101 years after the establishment of their osteopathic practice, Sister Anne Brooks, DO, put forth a challenge to her osteopathic peers to follow the founder of their profession.

Andrew Taylor Still was only too aware of the inadequacies of medical practice in his century. It challenged him enough that he became determined to look at medicine from a radically different angle. That he succeeded has been proven by the existence of our profession . . . as our second hundred years begins. We must take an "A. T. Still" view of the challenges and inadequacies of the medical practice of our day by looking at medicine from a radically different angle. . . . As osteopathic physicians living at the end of the twentieth century, I am challenging you to accept responsibility for change

RADICAL means taking away the pedestals on which physicians stand.

RADICAL means reforming the legal system.

RADICAL means making healthcare available to all, bringing justice and speed to reimbursement, and ending hassles with third-party payers.

RADICAL means keeping patients in good health and lowering costs. . . .

To meet this challenge, we have to educate our patients because we empower them when we do so. . . . The motto of osteopathic medicine in the twenty-first century should be Educate to Empower for Health. Education then becomes preventive medicine at its best, and we become prevention specialists. Prevention specialists are primary educators. . . . **We are the facilitators, not the healers.** . . . And lastly realize that our own lives also require preventive medicine. We must do the hardest thing in the world and look honestly at what our lifestyles are doing to ourselves and our families, friends and colleagues. [Emphasis mine; see appendix 5 for the entire address.]

◆ ◆ ◆

Sister Anne's life was full and her schedule extremely demanding—unpredictable hours when she was in Tutwiler, and tight travel arrangements with long waits in unfamiliar airports when presenting papers and attending meetings and conferences. But, along with the many positive ways she employed her personal power in response to the needs of others, Sister Anne recognized her soul's need for re-creation in quiet, personal time. Through her network of professional connections and caring friends and sisters, other doctors in private practice who wanted to help serve the poor in Tutwiler came to take her place as the attending doctor at the clinic for a week or two. Very grateful, Anne could go off schedule and recharge at a religious retreat or spend a couple of days with her religious director, Father Bill Moriarty, her trusted counselor in Chicago. With him she would "seek spiritual direction talk things through," and discuss her ideas.

And then, once a year, Anne had a real vacation—a restorative, relaxing time when her daily commitments and professional obligations took a holiday. She traveled to the Berkshires to enjoy a full week with good friends at their country estate, which was only a twenty-minute drive from Tanglewood, the famed summer home for the Boston Symphony Orchestra. For Anne, there was no better way to spend a summer evening than listening to Beethoven or Stravinsky or another one of the great classical composers' creations, played by professional musicians, in Tanglewood's massive open-air theater surrounded by a huge, lush lawn and verdant woods. Away from Tutwiler, the clinic, and the twenty-four/seven demands on her professional, emotional and spiritual strengths, as well as her time, she completely relaxed with cherished, simpatico souls in their secluded mountain retreat. She slept late if she felt like it and took leisurely walks through the natural beauty of the gentle rolling hills surrounding the house. On other evenings, she enjoyed gourmet dinners prepared by Marcus, the live-in cook, and the stimulating company of other dinner guests. One of her fondest memories was dining with Itzhak Perlman, the world-renowned violinist/conductor.

When Marcus knew Anne was coming, he always made her a huge welcome cookie. In his free time while she was there, he regaled her with stories about other guests or updates about what he had learned about her ancestors. Researching genealogy was his hobby. A story Anne still laughs about is when Marcus had churned-up a tub of homemade ice cream for dinner when Supreme Court Justice Ruth Bader Ginsburg was visiting. After serving dinner and dessert, he decided to put the remaining ice cream in the freezer that was in the barn behind the house. It was pitch-black dark as he went through the kitchen door, but since he was so familiar with the path, he didn't bother with a light. About halfway to the barn, Marcus was tackled. The Secret Service man, who helped him up, apologized when he saw that what might have been a bomb was a tub half full of ice cream.

Chapter Sixteen

THE RIPPLE EFFECT

Never worry about numbers. Help one person at a time, and always
start with the person nearest you.
—Mother Teresa

How does one begin to comprehend the incredible impact this one
life has made? The cover story article by Terry Hickey in the June
2003 edition of the *Magazine of Catholic Missionary Work in America*
summarized some of Sister Anne's remarkable accomplishments.
When the clinic opened in 1983, word traveled fast throughout Tallahatchie County about the care given at the Tutwiler Clinic. In the
first month of operation, 265 patients were treated. Twenty years later,
in 2003, Sister Anne and her staff treated an average of 750 patients
a month, nearly 9,000 patients a year—almost a threefold increase.

In those twenty years the clinic's actual size had also substan-
tially increased, with four additions to the original building and a
satellite clinic in Glendora, sixteen miles away. Their full array of
services provided general treatment, physical therapy, EKGs, x-rays,
laboratory services, eye exams, and dental care to people living in a
fifteen-county area. The staff had more than doubled, from twelve
people to twenty-nine—including two medical assistants who had
earned their s through a program offered by the clinic. Because Sister Anne was an adjunct professor at her alma mater, the Michigan
State University College of Osteopathic Medicine, the clinic usually

had one or two resident interns from there, plus other osteopathic colleges. "We have the best staff in the whole world," she said. "They are so caring . . . so dedicated." Sister Anne had turned sixty-five in 2003, and when asked if she had plans to retire, she responded, "I'm having too much fun. Why should I leave? This is my home."

Beyond the thousands of patients who received exceptional medical care at the clinic, the article in *Extension* magazine states, "the additional benefits that Anne Brooks initiated for that impoverished town during those first twenty years were best described in small measures—more than forty-five women had received their GEDs, Habitat for Humanity was building a new house a year, almost 175 children and teens were participating in afterschool programs, and Dr. Brooks's home was no longer serving as a make-shift emergency room, which she took as a sign that her patients were taking better care of their health."

However, although progress had been made, she strongly emphasized the needs were still great. Transportation, housing, educational opportunities, and jobs were desperately needed in Tutwiler. Behind this growth and glowing success was the ever-present reality that this small regional clinic relied on a national base of donors to meet its $1.6 million annual budget. Medicaid and Medicare payments accounted for about 22 percent of the clinic's income. It was up to Sister Anne and the other sisters to find the rest. These donations not only paid for the medical services received but also paid for the medicines prescribed. Sister Anne firmly believed in her "Pearly Gates Insurance Policy." She often said, "When I get to the Pearly Gates, I could never tell St. Peter I refused to treat anyone because he or she did not have the money to pay." Cindy Herring said, "Her mission was to give anyone who came to her the best possible medical care, even when it involved sending someone to a specialist. She would pay for anything out of her heart." That was the reason she so desperately needed donations and became a stellar fundraiser. And by the early 2000s, money was tight.

The *60 Minutes* program that aired in 1990, plus the surge of national newsprint and magazine features at that time, had helped the clinic expand its services as the needed financial support literally poured in. A savings account had been established, and much of the funds were invested to help with future needs. However, it was almost thirteen years since the clinic had been in that media spotlight, and the list of twenty-one thousand donors generated from all of the earlier publicity had dwindled to around six thousand. While constant, well-organized, and grateful attention was given to those faithful donors, the lifeblood of the clinic, the sisters were exceedingly thankful when in 2003 the *60 Minutes* program aired an update to its earlier Tutwiler Clinic program, and they once again saw an increase in their list of donors.

Donations came in from foundations and philanthropic organizations across the land, as well as individual parishioners in churches like St. Michael Church in St. Michael, Minnesota. According to an article in the same issue of the *Extension* magazine, which featured Sister Anne on the cover:

> Only a scant handful of the parishioners at St. Michael Church have ever had the chance to visit and see first hand the good work done at Sister Anne Brooks' medical clinic in Tutwiler, Mississippi. Most of the parishioners there knew about the ministry in that Delta town, almost 900 miles directly south on the Mississippi River [only] through the newsletter that the clinic sends out three times a year—and through the regular thank-yous that are sent out in between.
>
> . . . The 1,660 families in the parish have faithfully supported the clinic's work since 1985 . . . during the second weekend of the month we announce that the collection will be shared with the three mission projects that the parish supports on an on-going basis: a local food pantry, a mission in Guatemala and the Tutwiler Mission. Loose money in the collection is earmarked for those special projects, and in good economic times and in bad, the parishioners have come through with generous donations . . .

In a recent interview Sister Anne spoke about other sources: "There were individual donations from people who just care. One woman sent us her tips. Another guy got a job and sent us half his first paycheck. There's this marvelous outpouring of help from people all over the country who care." Cindy Herring recounted, "Friends and supporters from across the United States and around the world—Canada, England, Africa—some who have never met Dr. Brooks, continue to give 'til they die and then leave a substantial bequest in appreciation for the unique care Sister Anne Brooks provided."

◆ ◆ ◆

And the power of Dr. Anne Brooks's approach to medical care reached far beyond the boundaries of Tallahatchie County. On May 8, 2017, the nationwide contribution to her profession was recognized when she received Michigan State University College of Osteopathic Medicine's highest honor—the Walter F. Patenge Medal of Public Service.

◆ ◆ ◆

The lifeblood of the clinic is the donations of money and service from individuals like that pragmatic businessman Carl Mungenast, who heard the *60 Minutes* broadcast back in 1990 and was so impressed with Anne Brooks. He recently said, "That amazing woman. When I told other people her story and what she was doing in Tutwiler, they, too, were impressed and wanted to help and sent her a check. Now, over 30 years later, they still send her a check. My family, my kids got caught up in my passion. They started collecting things for the clinic's Bargain Barn to take down to Tutwiler in a rented truck twice a year. A cousin heard the story and said, 'Hey, I have a truck. I'll take you down when you want to go.' The circle kept getting larger. Other friends were collecting old clothes to clean and mend to send to the Tutwiler's Bargain Barn."

Mungenast continued, "At a party recently, a doctor who I knew years ago, and had moved out of town, came up to me and asked,

'How's your girlfriend in Tutwiler? I've never forgotten what you told me about her and still send her money.' Other friends collected old bicycles, broke them down and rebuilt them to send to Tutwiler. This made me stop to realize I have told her story to over a hundred people who send her money. It's Anne Brooks's dedication and spirit that hooks these people. I send the money because of her. She is the reason. [Now that she has retired], the clinic must keep her spirit alive. When I retired I was doing some consulting but did not want to fool with the taxes if I charged, so I always gave the client an envelope and said if you want to pay me, send a contribution to the Tutwiler Clinic. It can be a tax deduction for you."

◆ ◆ ◆

Sister Anne Brooks's mission depended on the support and compassion of these donors and their contributions to the clinic. She worked and prayed hard so that every individual who contributed would feel a deep commitment and personal connection to her and their shared mission. The newsletter the *Tutwiler Clinic and Outreach* was a powerful instrument for fundraising. It was sent to thousands of current, past, and potential donors three times a year—spring, summer, and fall. The eight pages of every newsletter were filled with the clinic's activities—photographs of volunteers, staff, and medical students, reports of the clinic and community center's programs, testimonials from patients and their families, and a list of medical needs. The fall issue usually had a holiday/Christmas wish list compiled for the children.

The newsletter was crafted to make each recipient feel directly connected to Sister Anne and her work. The lead article of every issue was a folksy, personal note signed by her and accompanied by her smiling photo, always in her white doctor's jacket, a stethoscope around her neck. These personalized notes, grounded in her deep faith, were often enlivened with a bit of her quirky sense of humor.

In the newsletter's opening message and in *Doctor Rounds*, the other column Sister Anne wrote, were moving descriptions of her patients' lives and problems. This is where she spilled out what was on her heart. These words give extraordinary insight into the personality, care, and faith of this remarkable woman.

Here are a few examples:

Spring 2004
To All You Wonderful Friends of the Tutwiler Clinic
It is windy today, 18 knots, the weatherman said, bringing in more rain. The fields look like one great big wetland and we were surprised last week to see the mud turning white with the sweeping arrival of countless geese. I cannot help but think of how your loving concern sweeps into our tiny corner of this land. You enable us to nourish and empower others whose lives of hardship begin to change into lives of hope—they realize someone really does care about them. That is truly a springtime event, the starting of a new life, a resurrection.

Fall 2001 (just after 9/11)
To All Our Dear Friends of the Tutwiler Clinic
Like yourselves, we have been deeply touched by the events of the past few months. We have been humbled by those of you who quickly shared your tax rebate checks with us, and by the many donations we have received in memory of the loved ones gone, or the firefighters or the clean-up crews of New York. Always, you are reaching beyond yourselves, trying to relieve the troubles of others by lending a helping hand. . . . It is this solidarity, these shared concerns that have allowed us to become a part of one family . . . which stretches even beyond the borders of our country.

Sister Anne's thoughts and prayers were never far from the tragic racism that shaped the community in which she now served, and she took every opportunity to remind "her friends."

Summer 2011

To All Our Dear Friends of the Tutwiler Clinic:

Dear Y'all,

This year is the 50th anniversary of the Freedom Riders—they risked their very lives to come to the South and help register voters....There is something so sacred about someone caring so very much about another person whom they never met—sacrifices made possible what seemed unobtainable, memories seared into one's heart are now embellished by the truth of that successful effort—success that is still in progress, because change rarely happens in a hurry.....you have been our "freedom riders" as it were—sacrificing your talents, your income, your time to make it possible for someone to enjoy improved health—efforts by total strangers to bring about change so lives can be saved, extended and lived more fully because YOU cared. What a gift!

Always mindful of maintaining a strong connection with her "friends," she typically opened her personal note with a light note of humor and closed with her message of deep faith:

Fall 2014

To All You Wonderful Friends of the Tutwiler Clinic, Inc.

It's Thanksgiving! This is my favorite season of the year—a time of scanning my soul, my heart, my brain—(and of course our computers!) so we can power up again the connections between us—your concern about our patients and how we can take care of them when they cannot pay, and our great, immeasurable gratitude to you, who consistently enable us to do mini-(and sometimes maxi-) miracles in this corner of Mississippi.

How grateful we are! And what a delightful feeling it is! This is a union of caring for those in need—and I personally think it nourishes and encourages us on our staff as much as it does you, back home. That warmth that seeps into our hearts (and of course, into our patients' hearts) gives all of us a big boost of energetic joy in a world that often appears very troubled and sad.

This encouragement to change our part of the world, even in the tough circumstances that we are aware of, comes from the Almighty One to whom we pray, and who responds by returning many blessings to you and all those dear to you, wrapping us all in love that has no end. And so from all of us. to all of you—THANK YOU AGAIN AND AGAIN.

Our love to you!

Sister Anne Brooks DO and staff

◆ ◆ ◆

"Doctor's Rounds" was the other column in every edition of the Tutwiler Clinic newsletter written by Sister Anne. Here, small vignettes about the patients she saw in her daily practice helped keep the readers informed and intimately engaged with the clinic's primary mission.

This column always gave a sample of the distressing challenges, heart-wrenching experiences, and brave and warm humanity that she encountered daily.

Fall 2000

Doctor's Rounds

He was lying on the bench in front of the clinic when I drove by to go to the hospital for early morning rounds. When I returned I discovered he had walked about 10 miles before he caught a ride to the Clinic. He was worried he said, because of his foot, but it didn't hurt, it just looked bad. He took off his worn sneaker, lifted his pants leg, and there was a great open ulcer down almost to the bone. Thin, his skin dry, his diabetes poorly controlled, he reluctantly allowed me to persuade him to go to the hospital for nourishment and care.

◆ ◆ ◆

I sat in the twilight beside her bed and twined my fingers with hers. "It looks like it might be cancer," I said. I watched her face. No change of expression. "I kind of thought so," she said, and smiled a little nervously. She didn't look 82. Somehow, in spite of my own birthdays, patients weren't supposed to get older. I thought of the many beautiful flowers she had brought to the clinic, the cookies she stashed on my desk. I didn't want to be saying these words to her. I just wanted her pain to go away. "It's ok," she said. "God won't let me down. And if my heart stops, just let me go." Her quiet wisdom and her calm faith seemed to fill the room, enfolding us with peace. We just stayed there together, wondering, praying for a long, long time, bordering eternity.

◆ ◆ ◆

"Naw, I ain't been to a doc in 35 years!" I looked at his beet-red face, figuring it had to be something bad to bring him in the day before the 4th of July. He couldn't tell me what hurt. He just didn't feel right. At 56, he had been farming most of his life, And yes, he liked his beer. A high white blood count signaled infection, but his swollen red tonsils would not have raised it that much. And no, he "warn't goin to no hospital." We gave him a shot of the strongest antibiotic we had. I made him promise to return after the holiday. On the 4th the ER called. He had come in, vomiting. I ran up the road to the hospital, found him with a tight, tense, belly. The surgeon wouldn't cut until he had a supply of matching blood that had to come from Jackson, 3 hours away. Just before midnight the surgeon called. "His whole belly is full of necrotizing fasciitis!" Ominous, those big words, terrifying to doctors and basically saying he was rotting from "flesh eating bacteria." Shortly, he was placed on the helicopter and carried to the university hospital in Memphis, his distraught family following by car. Sadly, in spite of everything, his kidneys failed and he died about 10 days later.

◆ ◆ ◆

At my request she stood on the chair beside her new brother, who was lying on the pediatric exam table, tiny, round, energetic, hollering indignantly at being displaced from his mama's arms. She [his big sister] gravely looked into his ears with me, listened to his heart beat. She held his hand "so he won't get scared." But she drew the line at looking in his throat, shaking her braids with their pretty beads. "Ugh!" she said. "That where the food goes down the drain!"

And when there was an impressive victory, Anne Brooks was the first to share it with her friends in this column:

Fall 2015

Doctor's Rounds

He was finally put in the nursing home after his terrible accident in August of 2011. Mostly semiconscious for many weeks, when I would visit him, each morning he had been turned on his left side so that he could see the photos of his children taped to his bed rail. V e r y, v e r y slowly his body began to try to heal, but his mind was elsewhere. I worried about his future—could he ever go back home? By 2013 he was able to transfer to the rehab center; and nurses lined the hall, clapping, as the supervisor proudly pushed his wheelchair to the waiting vehicle. . . . It was 2015 that he came to the Clinic, verbal, joking, proudly managing an electric wheelchair. He was grinning from ear to ear as he reached into his pocket and handed me a laminated business card.

THERE IT WAS! His diploma!

In the newsletter was a copy of the diploma, signed by all the dignitaries.

ALCORN STATE UNIVERSITY
JOSEPH JUDE II
MASTER OF SCIENCE IN SECONDARY EDUCATION
on the
TWELFTH DAY OF MAY TWO THOUSAND AND FIFTEEN

◆ ◆ ◆

AFTERWORD

Be Who You Is!
—Ms. Rosie, an elderly, beloved art student at the Tutwiler Community Education Center

On June 15, 2017, hundreds of well wishers—doctors, hospital and clinic staffs, current and former patients, students, and friends—crowded into the Delta Blues Museum in Clarksdale to honor Dr. Anne Brooks at a reception hosted by Merit Health of Northwest Mississippi (formerly known as the Clarksdale Hospital). Dr. Brooks was retiring. On June 4, 2017, she had turned seventy-nine. Although her spirit was as strong as ever, if not stronger, her stamina and health were feeling those years. In a lengthy, heartfelt decision, she had determined it was time to "take down her shingle" and move into a new phase of her life. She would move to be among her sisters at St. Joseph's Provincial House, located in Latham, New York. It had been sixty years since the spring of 1957 when Sister Anne Eucharista Brooks had taken her vows to become a nun. At the announcement of her retirement, her Catholic family also had wanted to express their love and admiration for her life of service. In the spring of 2017, they held a large celebration in her honor that was attended by two bishops, multitudes of her church friends, and members of the Catholic clergy.

During the first week of July 2017, Sister Anne said good-bye to the Tutwiler Clinic, Tallahatchie County, and the Mississippi Delta.

◆ ◆ ◆

Sister Anne Brooks's middle name is Eucharista, the Greek word for communion, and Sister Anne has an incredible gift for communion—creating connection. This is her power. Even now in retirement at St. Joseph's Provincial House and no longer in active practice, she has not lost her ability to connect at a deep level with someone in need. In a recent conversation she shared her joy of holding the hand of one of the other resident nuns by giving comfort to that sister during her final hours. In the residential halls of her new home, she is a compassionate presence, ever aware of and responsive to the needs of others.

And Sister Anne never limited her understanding to her contemporaries. She creates a connection to all ages. Jason Jones, Carl Mungenast's grandson, appreciated her knowing concern in a very different way. Several years ago, when Jason graduated from high school in Moline, Illinois, he and a friend bought a very old, delivery-type, panel truck and set off to visit family and friends in other parts of the country. Jason's grandfather said, "One of their stops was to be in Tutwiler with an offer to do some handyman work for a day or two. Sister Brooks put them to work but knew they might get bored not knowing the area. She knew teenaged boys might like music, girls, and youthful fellowship. So, she directed them to some of the places in Clarksdale where they could have a good time." Jason and his friend had a great time and marveled that Sister Anne would even know of such spots.

◆ ◆ ◆

One of Sister Anne's most cherished treasures at her new home in Latham, New York, is a big grey rock that was splashed with color and signed by her colleagues, staff, and friends at her farewell reception in Clarksdale, Mississippi. A rock absolutely symbolizes the remarkable power of Sister Anne Brooks, DO. A rock thrown into a pool of water creates a circle of ripples. As that circle expands, some of the ripples break away to produce more ripples, which will eventually break away to create more and more ripples.

This is Anne Brooks's legacy. Her amazing power, dogged determination, deep faith, and extraordinary love that brought light to
Tallahatchie County now continues to create many, many ripples of
inspiration and holistic understanding against some of the darker
powers that haunt our world.

ACKNOWLEDGMENTS

This book is in many ways a personal memoir of Sister Anne Brooks, DO, because her words present so much of the story. And what a privilege it has been to share the many hours of conversation with her, both in person and on the phone, plus reading her past speeches, interviews, and personal papers. Our deepest gratitude goes first to Sister Anne, who, in a delightfully open way, graciously shared the story of her life.

In early June of 2017, I received a phone call from Panny Mayfield, a noted photographer and writer from the Mississippi Delta, who asked if I would consider undertaking writing the story of the remarkable Anne Brooks, the Catholic nun and osteopathic physician who had been the medical director of the Tutwiler Clinic for thirty-four years. Panny had known Sister Anne ever since the doctor had moved to Tutwiler. Panny always intended to write Sister Anne's story but was currently covered over with multiple obligations and would not have the time for the writing for several years. This presented a problem. Sister Anne was retiring at the end of June and moving to New York. When Panny shared her dilemma with Sister Anne, she suggested that since I'd written another book situated in the Delta (*Delta Rainbow: The Irrepressible Betty Bobo Pearson*), I might be interested.

They wanted my answer as soon as possible. The next week my husband and I drove the ninety-plus miles from Memphis to Tutwiler to meet with Sister Anne and Panny. We spent a couple of hours, and it didn't take me long to realize that here was an amazing, compelling, uplifting story about a remarkable woman. Panny, who had been documenting Sister Anne's time in Tutwiler, loaded the four large cartons of files and publications from the trunk of her car to the back of my Subaru, and I called Jean Fisher, who collaborated with me on

Delta Rainbow. I wanted us to partner on the Anne Brooks story and Jean agreed. We flew to Latham, New York, for two days of intensive conversation with Anne and had many phone interviews after that.

Panny Mayfield was our first interview after Anne. Other key interviews we conducted in person or by phone over the next four months were with Sister Cora Lee Middleton, RN, a housemate of Dr. Brooks and her medical right hand at the clinic; Sister Maureen Delaney, who was the key to the successful outreach programs and the establishment of the Tutwiler Community Center; Sister Mary Bertoli, who taught art at the Tutwiler Community Center and captured enchanting scenes from the Mississippi Delta in tissue-paper collage; Cindy Herring, Dr. Brooks's administrative assistant, who found an answer to every question we asked; Betty Barbieri, who handles the clinic's financial records, Genether Spurlock, first a volunteer and then a program director at the Community Center, and Betty Pearson, a Mississippi Delta plantation owner, neighbor, and patient of Sister Anne's.

Our good friend Laura Robinson, who is a member of the Catholic Church, introduced us to Father Art Kirwin, who shared some of the basic history, organizational structure, and outreach of the Catholic Church in Mississippi. Joan Terry, another Catholic friend, recommended readings for us to better understand a nun's spiritual commitments. Writer Susan Cushman was an initial reader of our early drafts. Josh Howard, the producer of the original *60 Minutes* program, willingly shared tales of his ongoing friendship with Sister Anne over the years and was very enthusiastic about the book, as was Carl Mungenast, who regularly called from St. Louis to check on our progress and feed us additional information.

A big thank-you also goes to Craig Gill and Lisa McMurtray at the University Press of Mississippi, whose guidance has been invaluable, plus the readers with the press who made some very helpful organizational recommendations. And a huge thank-you goes to John Thomason, who has given his editorial advice, personal support, and encouragement throughout the whole process.

Appendix 1

POETIC MUSINGS

Among the many personal papers that Sister Anne shared for the writing of this book, some were musings, captured in a poetic voice—a voice so different from the soft, understanding tones she used to communicate with her patients and, more different still, from the professional language, which sounds like a foreign tongue to anyone other than a fellow physician. Such words, probably penned in the middle of the night and later transcribed to type on a sheet of white paper, give voice to hopes, frustrations, longings, pain, thankfulness, and questions.

Most of her writings have no date. Could this have been penned as she entered medical school?

Lord God,
My Carissime—
today I hear You say
that You have already prepared Your plans for me,
Even though I might not yet be ready—
Plans for a future
I many not even want to think about yet . . .
Maybe
Because I haven't gathered up my hopes yet?
Maybe Because I am afraid?

I only know I am a wimp without you
and
that in my future
You must be there with me all the time or I won't make it!
And I guess,

Judging by these many years I have already lived,
I should already know for sure
That you will place close to me
folks specially chosen by You:
wonderful, caring, delightful, wise people
who will walk with me,
and help shape my life
by bringing me / keeping me
ever closer to You . . .
What a future!
How can I be afraid and worried?

Others voice the pain in her heart, as she remembers what she can't forget after she came to Tutwiler:

Terrance

Sudden blinding headlights
Staccato blaring horn
Frantic pounding hand

And
Fumbling for glasses
Unlocking outside door
Teen mom terrified

Verified
Limp 4 month old body
Feeding tube leaking
Carefully swaddled
Laid on my crumpled bed

Dead
Heart sounding silent
Pupils now unseeing
Lungs filled with feeding

Pleading
No room for air

No pulse ignited
No breath stirred

Heard
Weeping, wailing
Keening, sobbing
Lamentation

Aspiration
Born cord first
Sucking absent
Muscles frozen

Chosen
Cherished
Treasured
Loved forever

However
This dawn
Returned to God
So reluctantly

In 1999, after living and working in the Mississippi Delta for sixteen years, Doctor Brooks had prepared a comprehensive report of the Tutwiler area and penned the following reflection to capture her feeling for the Delta and its people:

I have chosen cotton as a symbol.
In its beauty,
It reflects the ambiguity of the Delta.
It must be planted
When the soil is the right temperature.
A fringed triangle (called a square)
Brings forth an ivory flower,
Which becomes pink on the third day.

A closed boll grows
When the flower dies.
In the heat it matures and pops to reveal the fiber.

The life-giving leaves are removed
So it can be harvested:

A cause of slavery and oppression
A source of livelihood and wealth
A source of clothing, food, and innumerable uses.

It is tough.
It is beautiful. It is mesmerizing.
Like the Delta and its people.

In a piece dated Christmas A.D. 2011, Sister Anne explored her faith within the science of the stars.

What Was It Like?

What was it like,
O God, Creator of the seemingly infinite universe,
To choose the Star of Bethlehem timeless eons before the earth was formed
Would be a perfect co-incidence for the birth of your Son?
And what was it like,
O amorphous cloud of interstellar gases,
To birth a light-bearing mass from the inky-ness of the black-hole-depths of
space
Specifically to honor the King of Kings?

And what was it like,
O Sun,
To allow gravity to form, in this universe,
To rein in your planets,
To measure the perfect distance for life to form
And to hear God call you to rule over the Day on this yet-to-be perfect world
Where God would walk in the cool of the evening, and later in the heat of the
day?

And what was it like,
O World,
When people were formed from the mud of the earth,
Molded by the loving hands of God,

Life-breath transmitted into them by the Spirit of God,
Interstellar dust in their sinews and bones,
And yet who failed to obey their Creator,
Allowing evil to attempt to try to change civilization?

And you,
O Star of Wonder,
Your light speeding through space,
What did you think of how the stage was being set
For a Redeemer
For these troubled and battered people?

And what was it like,
O Star, when that wondrous night finally arrived in the Fullness of Time?
Did you see His mom? Did you see Him? Was He cute?
And did you dance for joy?

And you,
O Star of Night,
Did you see the Magi pointing at you, night after night, mile after mile after
mile?
And did you hear the murmuring about your beauty
And pondering your reason to be there?
And what did you think of that dangerous journey you guided them on
So they could see what you had seen?

And what has happened to you,
O Starlight, which reached our world that night?
You didn't go out, like the flame of a candle—
Your source of Light continues burning on.

Instead, you keep on shining even now, into our own lives,
Giving our civilization an inheritance to treasure
So that we see the light tonight that saw God's only Son
And now we know that
We must look with God's Eyes
And listen with God's Ears
And love with God's Heart, which is beating in our hearts,
And do God's Work on this Earth in such a way

That it will become as bright as your light,
As eternal as your light
Full of praise for God, Whose children we are
And who can live forever, endless as your light, eternal as our God . . .

◆ ◆ ◆

When Sister Maureen departed from the clinic in 2015, Sister Anne, honoring and celebrating the accomplishments of another, drew on her creative voice to write a farewell column that was published in the fall issue of the clinic's newsletter:

A very special person joined us in Tutwiler in 1987. By helping local folks recognize how important their ideas were, how to figure out what was the best way they could accomplish dreams they had never thought possible, and yes, enable hidden gifts to come to light—this person, sister Maureen Delaney, listened to the folks and their needs and ideas and helped them bring to life the seeds of possibilities dormant for years in their hearts and minds.

A meeting place? When the library said "No!" an ancient town building was rebuilt with YOUR help, and became the Tutwiler Community Education Center.

The town is a mess! Well, Sister Maureen listened and encouraged folks to come together to figure out what was needed—a town cleanup with an integrated celebration and with trophies for the most trash and cleanest places. And speeches, of course! And food, and chatting with people you seldom had a chance to speak to! And the high school band played—and spirits soared . . .

The town bayou flooding up into homes? We'll call in the Army Corps of Engineers!

Let's learn how to write poetry! And a special meeting introduced new young poets who read their works to assembled relatives and friends. What talent!

Quilting! Teen helpers! A full gym, basketball games with neighboring counties!

Candidates' night at voting time! How to take good photos! Senior Wednesdays! A wellness program! Zumba lessons! Supervised computer time for students! The list is impressively wonderful . . .

Now we send Sister Maureen off to her new career—she is the newly elected leadership head of the US–Ontario Province of the Sisters of the Holy Names, which is my religious community also.

To you, sister Maureen, we give our great gratitude for all you have done in our little corner of the world, all you have enabled us to accomplish. And our fervent prayers of blessing go with you that God will hold you close and keep us always in your heart.

With loving gratitude from all of us,

—Sister Anne Brooks DO and staff

Appendix 2

AWARDS AND HONORS

1975   Service to Mankind Award—Northwest Florida Sertoma Club

1977   Key to the City of St. Petersburg, Florida—Mayor Schuh
Key to the City of Clearwater, Florida—Mayor Gabe

1981   Service to Immokalee Migrants Award—Collier Health Services, Inc.

1987   Award for Service in the Health Field—Mississippi Religious Leadership Conference
Phillips Medal of Public Service—Ohio University of Osteopathic Medicine, Athens, Ohio
Alumnus of the Year Award—Michigan State University College of Osteopathic Medicine

1989   Alumni Service Award—Michigan State University, Lansing

1990   Norman Vincent Peale Award for Positive Thinking—presented by Dr. Peale, Los Angeles

1991   Meritorious Leadership Award—Tougaloo College, Jackson, Mississippi
Americans Award—presented at the John F. Kennedy Center, Washington, DC
Doctor of Humane Letters Honorary Degree—La Salle University, Philadelphia
Humanitarian Award—Auxiliary to the American Osteopathic Assoc., New Orleans

1992   Doctor of Medical Science Honorary Degree—Villanova University, Philadelphia
Inducted as a Fellow of the American Academy of Osteopathic Physicians, San Diego

Caring Award—presented by Caring Institute at US Capitol
and inducted into the Hall of Fame of Caring Americans at
Frederick Douglass Museum, Washington, DC

1993   Doctor of Laws Honorary Degree—Gonzaga University, Spokane,
Washington

1994   Taste of the South Award—Southern Congressional Delegation,
Washington, DC

1995   Doctor of Science Honorary Degree—University of New England
College of Osteopathic Medicine, Portland, Maine

1996   Nominated by Clarksdale and Six Counties Medical Society for
State Medical Assoc. Physician Service Award

1997   Martin Luther King, Jr. Award—International Fellowship of
Reconciliation, Alkmaar, the Netherlands
Doctor of Science Honorary Degree—Michigan State University, E.
Lansing
Widow's Mite Award—McCarthy Family Foundation

1998   Commitment and Devotion to Serving Humanity Award—
Tallahatchie Development League
Doctors Who Go the Extra Mile—Medical Economics Magazine

2000   One of the Delta's Top 75 Women in Business—Delta Business
Journal
Outstanding Business Development Efforts and Continuing
Contribution to the Overall Economic Advancement of the
State plaque—State of Mississippi Office of the Governor and
the Department of Economic and Community Development
Outstanding Catholic Woman of the Year—National Catholic
Daughters of America

2002   Doctor of Humane Letters honorary degree—University of
Medicine and Dentistry of New Jersey
Hero Medal for Demonstrating Integrity, Competency and
Vision as a Leader of the Osteopathic Profession—American
Osteopathic Association
An Award presented in Appreciation and Recognition of Her
Exceptional Leadership of Staff and Dedicated Service to the
Patients of the Mississippi Delta 2000–2002—Medical staff of
NW Regional Medical Center

2003   Physician of the Year—National Republican Congressional
Committee, Washington, DC [She says she doesn't know how
this happened—she's not a Republican.]

2004   Spirit of Humanity Award—American Foundation of Osteopathy
2005   Pride in the Profession Award—American Medical Association
        Foundation
2007   Award for Community Service—Mississippi Medical Association
        Honored for Years of Service to the Needy—Regional Medical
        Center Board of Trustees
        Distinguished Alumna Award—Barry University Alumni
        Association, Miami, FL
2008   Doctor of Humane Letters honorary degree—Des Moines
        University of Health Sciences, Des Moines, IA
        One of forty peer selected for Great Pioneers in Osteopathic
        Medicine Award—House of Delegates of American Osteopathic
        Association
        Honored for twenty-five years of service—the staff of Tutwiler
        Clinic
2009   Credited by Ivan Serto-Radies, MD, for assistance to him when he
        came to Tutwiler as a visiting Fulbright Scholar in 2002. (His
        goal was to learn about race relations because of the prejudice in
        his native Hungary against the Roma [Gypsies]. He received the
        State Dept. Alumni Award at the US Embassy in Budapest.)
        Finalist in nominations for the Robert Woods Johnson Community
        Health Leader Award
        Finalist in nominations for Kanter Prize from the Health Legacy
        Partnership, awarded $25,000 for Tutwiler Clinic
2010   Honored by the American Osteopathic Association at the House of
        Delegates Meeting
        Certificate of Appreciation awarded by the US Ontario Province
        Health and Well-Being Department of the Sisters of the Holy
        Names in gratitude for commitment to the love and care of the
        sisters.
2012   Nominated for CNN Heroes by Freddie Britt, president of
        Covenant Bank in Clarksdale, MS
        Honored at the 20th anniversary of the Tutwiler Community
        Education Center
        Physician of the Year Award—American Osteopathic Foundation
        Honored by the administration and staff of NW MS Regional
        Medical Center for Physician of the Year Award
2013   Nominated for the Lumen Christi Award—Catholic Diocese of
        Jackson, MS

2016   Honored as Top Physician in Tutwiler MS—International
        Association of Health Care Professionals (IAHCP), spotlighted
        in *The Leading Physicians of the World* publication
        Awarded the Honorary Degree of Humane Letters—Lincoln
        Memorial University
        Awarded the Henry Pace Service Award—William Carey University
        of Osteopathic Medicine
2017   The Walter F. Patenge Medal of Public Service—Michigan State
        University College of Osteopathic Medicine

Appendix 3

A TIMELINE FOUND IN
SISTER ANNE'S PAPERS

Born **1938**

Early years in non-Catholic family in Washington, DC. Father in Navy, alcoholic mother. Sent to Catholic boarding school in Florida age ten.

1955 Took vows. BS in education Barry University, Miami, Florida. Postgraduate work Univ. of Miami and Univ. of South Florida. Teacher and administrator—confined largely to wheelchair for fifteen years.

Professional experience: teaching and administration in elementary and junior high schools.

1982 Cured. Went to med school became a Doctor of Osteopathic Medicine, Michigan State University. Tuition from National Public Health Corps in exchange for four-year obligation to serve in needy poverty area.

Summer intern at École Européenne d'Ostéopathie, Maidstone, England and La Poizat, France.

1983 Sister Anne and three other Catholic nuns opened Tutwiler Clinic and eliminated segregated waiting areas in an empty building that was built with federal grant funds as part of the federal rural health initiative twenty years before. It had been closed for five years because of no doctor.

Rented for $1 a year from town of Tutwiler. Catholic Extensions provided $30,000, fourteen patients first day, seven hundred patients a month, twenty years later.

1985 Anne Brooks's story told in March 23, 1985, *People* magazine, an American weekly magazine of celebrity and human-interest stories, published by Time Inc., with a readership of 46.6 million adults. Article reprinted to give to potential applicants to PHS (Public Health Services) practice.

Letter of congratulations from the United States Surgeon General, C. Everett Koop.

1987 Michigan State University College of Osteopathic Medicine *Alumnus of the Year*. Her obligation to the National Public Health Corps ended, but Sister Anne's dedicated service at the Tutwiler Clinic lasted an additional thirty years.

KKK warning left on Brooks's car windshield after she hired first black employee.

1990 September 23rd CBS *60 Minutes* "Profile of Anne Brooks," produced by Josh Howard. Brought in enough donations to build a new wing on the clinic.

John Vogel, director of purchasing of the Reading, Pennsylvania, hospital and medical center organized donations through his membership in the Pennsylvania Chapter of the American Society for Hospital Materials Management. One thousand dollars and a 45 ft tractor trailer full of supplies were sent to the [clinic]—surgery equipment, instruments, wheelchairs, cribs, linens, office supplies, furniture, latex gloves, IV sets, catheters, commode chairs, walkers, infant car seats, and much more.

Mildrette Graves, a gold medalist in the 1968 Olympic was gymnastics teacher for Community Center's summer program.

Tutwiler's quilters' products displayed at the Renwick Gallery of the Smithsonian Institution in Washington, DC.

1991 Jeff Piselli, news editor for the Clarksdale Press Register, canoed more than seven hundred miles down the muddy Mississippi from its source at Lake Itaasca, Minnesota, until he had to abort the trip near Dubuque, Iowa, because of family emergency. Piselli said the trip was "to do something good for a good cause, [gathering pledges and donations] for the Tutwiler Clinic."

1992 Brooks logged 9,200 patient visits this year, only half of them covered by Medicaid or Medicare.

1993 American Osteopathic Association convention—*Andrew Taylor Still Memorial Address.*

Gonzaga University, *Honorary Doctor of Laws.* Commencement address.

1994 The Society of St. Vincent de Paul—*Keynote speaker* at national convention.

1995 School of Osteopathic Medicine, Stratford, New Jersey. (nation's largest university of health sciences); Brooks gave *opening lecture in dean's series* to celebrate twenty-fifth anniversary.

The University of New England College of Osteopathic Medicine, Biddeford, Main—*commencement speaker/honorary doctorate of science.*

1997 The Baxter Allegiance Foundation cited Brooks as *A Local Hero.* Awarded clinic $50,000 with a future pledge of $25,000.

Clinical instructor for nurse practitioners-in-training from University of Mississippi for Women, University of Mississippi and University of Alabama; medical director and chief administrator Tutwiler Clinic; Mississippi preceptor for medical students-in-training from colleges of osteopathic medicine in Michigan, Texas, California, Pennsylvania, Ohio, Maine, West Virginia, and Illinois, and allopathic colleges of medicine in Mississippi, Wisconsin, and Iowa.

Martin Luther King, Jr. Peace Prize of $2,500 from the International Fellowship of Reconciliation.

1998 VP of medical staff Northwest Mississippi Regional Medical Center.

Tutwiler Clinic took in $276,000 from patient fees—Medicaid, Medicare, insurance, and self-pay patients. Had to raise $739,000 in donations across the world to keep the clinic open.

State Representative Tommy Reynolds introduced bill to make it easier for low-income Mississippians to qualify for drug coverage. Legislation passed, vetoed by governor.

Received Kellogg Foundation help for screening and management of high blood pressure and diabetes.

2000 Chosen *Catholic Woman of the Year* by the Catholic Daughters of America—received $10,000.

Recognized as one of *Delta's Top 75 Women in Business.*

Chief of Staff Northwestern Mississippi Regional Medical Center—first woman to hold this position.

2003 Twentieth anniversary of the clinic's opening. Bishop William Houck, president of Catholic Extension, congratulated Sister Anne "on this remarkable milestone. I don't think anyone imagined the kind of change that Sister Anne and the clinic would bring about. She is an example of how missionaries fill crucial voids across our country. We are grateful that we have been able to help her and her staff help the people of the Mississippi Delta for general treatment, physical therapy, EKGs, x-rays, laboratory services, eye exams and dental care to people living in a fifteen-county area."

Received $150,000 to date, through an ongoing tithing program from a parish in Minnesota.

Medicaid and Medicare payments account for only 25 percent of $1.6 million budget. Nine thousand patients per year. Staff of twenty-nine provide in addition to medical needs. Quilting circle helps patients socialize, earn income, and improve self-esteem. The other programs are reading classes, clothing exchange, emergency food requests, teen pregnancy prevention program, play group for two-to four-year-olds with mandatory parenting classes.

Satellite clinic in Glendora established.

June cover story of *Extension: Magazine of Catholic Missionary Work in America*—good article by Terry Hickey.

2004 Student doctor, Allison Hailman spent the month of December in training with Dr. Brooks. Hailman learned "the sickest patients have the best attitudes, and the poorest people are often poor because of illness and not being able to work. People subsist on disability and charity from family members. . . . Dr. Brooks is an amazing teacher and routinely teaches me from 7 a.m. to 7 p.m. She is one of the first to consistently work with me daily on SOAP notes, H&P's and EKG's. As a result, I feel much more confident in my physical exam skills and less scared of the Board exam! Dr. Brooks went all-out to teach me a little bit of everything. The nurses and office staff were supportive, helpful and friendly, too."

Cost of a patient visit: $168.80 (twenty-five salaries contribute to the overhead). Payment per patient visit $47.40.

2005 Michigan State University College of Osteopathic Medicine *graduation speaker.*

Sister Anne Marie Bucher, a massage therapist from New York, had come for ten years; and Jean Weisensee, an RN from Oregon, for twenty-two years, to volunteer their services to the clinic for a week each year.

2008 Des Moines University of Health Science awarded Anne Brooks the *Honorary Doctor of Humane Letters,* and she gave the commencement address.

In her keynote commencement address at the Ohio University College of Osteopathic Medicine she emphasized, *"Because you are a physician you will be expected to be able to do everything. But what you really need to do is care— really care."*

Everyone welcome at Tutwiler Clinic regardless of ability to pay. Only a third of town's 1,400 residents were employed—per capita income less than $3,000—Tallahatchie County was the poorest county in the nation.

2010 Visit from students and staff from Harvard University Center for Public Leadership to the Clinic.

2011 Dr. Narayan Bhetwal left after four years of service at Clinic.

New x-ray machine. Transitioning health records to new integrated system—21,000 charts.

Panelist at the Institute for the Advancement of Multicultural and Minority Medicine meeting in Washington, DC.

2012 Twentieth anniversary of Tutwiler Community Education Center

Commencement speaker for inaugural graduating class of Colorado Rocky Vista University College of Osteopathic Medicine.

2013 Dr. David Levine, DO, joined staff. Dr. Jimmy Humber, DO, came to clinic two afternoons each month to give vision exams

2014 Sister Rita D'Astous died; [. . .] with her sister Zenon, an RN, [she] joined sister Anne in the establishment of the clinic in 1983.

TV crews for interviews from Netherlands and Denmark.

Dr. Levine resigned. Dr. Nawal Shekhawaat joined staff. He said, "I am very impressed that the clinic is so well staffed. . . . The staff's intake is so thorough that I am able to spend quality time with each patient. More quality information allows me to give a better diagnosis and makes it easier to manage patient care. At this clinic it is all about the quality of care given to each patient."

At Christmas a generous donor made it possible for Tutwiler families to get items they could most use, at a JC Penny store forty miles away—socks, shoes, underwear, towels, p.j.s nightgowns, men's shirts, shorts, flip-flops, bowls, household supplies, baby items, school uniforms, slippers, kids' Ts, shorts, hoodies, etc., etc., etc. . .

1,087 Donors!

2015 Sherwin Williams's donors and volunteers painted four houses that were built twenty-five years before behind the clinic for families who lived in the Tutwiler flood zone where the much-polluted bayou often heavily overflowed.

Ryan Hagensen, a third-year medical student from William Carey University College of Osteopathic Medicine in Hattiesburg, Mississippi, spent a month in Tutwiler with Dr. Anne Brooks as his preceptor. "My time here has been a blessing. One that will always be set apart from my other rotations simply because the Tutwiler Clinic is unique . . . The Clinic is 'unique' in the lengths that the staff here goes to make sure each patient is cared for. That may include providing transportation to appointments, filing prescriptions that would otherwise be unaffordable, providing clothing or other personal needs or simply being a friend. 'Unique" in that nowhere else have I found such a group of dedicated people who show so much love and kindness. . . . Dr. Brooks has given me a much better impression of what being a physician is and should be."

New very expensive chemistry analyzer came from an anonymous donor.

For twenty-eight years women in Tutwiler and the surrounding area produced 22,000 hand-quilted pot holders, 1,700 quilts, as well as bags, placemats, wall hangings and table runners to sell to the public. The Tutwiler Center provided the materials and purchased the item from the quilter to sell in Clarksdale at the Delta Blues Museum and the Shack Up Inn.

2016 Tornados and floods in Tutwiler. Town bridge under five feet of water.

Gave commencement address at DeBusk College in Cumberland Gap, Tennessee, and the final blessing to third graduating class of Doctor of Osteopathic College at William Carey University in Hattiesburg, Mississippi.

To date, forty-one Habitat Homes have been built in Tutwiler by volunteers from across the nation, with houses #42 and #43 under construction.

Tallahatchie General Hospital purchased Tutwiler Clinic after thirty-three years. The clinic had a staff of thirty-two.

Sister Joann Blomme, counselor at the clinic for many years, accepted a call for a new position elsewhere. She taught youngsters manners at MacDonald's, took teenagers to Walmart for swimsuits that would "fit," played with kids on office rug while their mom was in medical examination, counseled teens and depressed adults.

Marilyn and Jim Martell made seventy-first trip from Milwaukee with a van full of items for the Bargain Barn, program materials and treats for the community center, and medical supplies.

Dr. Shekhawat left Tutwiler Clinic to become a hospitalist at the Baptist Conway Hospital in Conway, Arkansas.

Dorothy Dodd, who served the Clinic as a van driver and housekeeper since 1986, retired.

The spring newsletter does not mention Dr. Sister Anne Brooks's retirement, but her last day at the Clinic was June 30, 2017.

Appendix 4

A CHRONICLE OF
CIVIL RIGHTS EVENTS

Gathered by S. Anne Brooks, DO, Tutwiler Clinic
in Her First Twenty-Five Years in Tutwiler, Mississippi

Also found in Sister Anne's private papers was a lengthy, more scholarly piece. She had kept the following timeline of the civil rights movement, starting with the murder of Emmett Till.

◆ ◆ ◆

Between 1882 and 1968, 4,709 lynchings occurred in forty-three states.

1954

The case of *Brown vs. Board of Education* decision declared segregation in public schools unconstitutional.

1955

Mar. 23: Jackson Citizens Council chartered as a nonprofit corporation.

Aug. 28: Emmett Till, a Chicago fourteen-year-old, was accused of whistling at a white woman while he was buying candy in a store in Money owned by JW Milam and attended by his wife, Carolyn. His body was found by a fisherman three days later in the Tallahatchie River, chained to a gin fan. He had been beaten beyond recognition and had been shot in the head. Among Tutwiler Clinic patients involved in the Emmett Till case is Woodrow Jackson, who embalmed his body. Mr. Jackson said,

"I'm proud of what I did. It's hard to do a wet body, and they wanted the casket open." The funeral was held in Chicago. Another patient, recently deceased, was JW Kellum, lawyer for the defense, who said, "When they heard it was a Federal case, they wanted every lawyer in the county." Mr. Kellum's photo appeared in the *Look* magazine article at the time. Harvey Henderson, another local lawyer, died in 2007. The trial was held in Sumner Courthouse. The all-white jury, after deliberating for an hour and five minutes, did not find JW Milam and Roy Bryant guilty, but they were shunned by their neighbors and moved away. (See 2007.)

Dec. 1: Rosa Parks refused to give up her seat on the bus to a white man and was arrested. (See 1999.)

1956

The Mississippi Sovereignty Commission was formed by the state legislature to preserve segregation laws in the state.

1957

Aug.: Congress passed the Civil Rights Act.

1958

Sept. 22: The Citizens' Council, Inc., was chartered as part of [a] white supremacy group.

1959

Apr. 25: Mack Charles Parker, a truck driver, was accused of raping a white woman in Poplarville. He was dragged from his jail cell by a lynch mob. He was shot, bound in chains and his body thrown into the Pearl River. No one was ever charged or punished.

Dr. Gilbert Mason, Dr. Felix Dunn, Eulice White, and Joseph Austin petitioned Harrison County supervisors to allow blacks access to the beach. When denied, they organized a series of wade-ins. Riots followed, with six blacks and one white being shot. The beach was finally opened nine years later.

1960

Dr. Aaron Henry, a pharmacist from Clarksdale, was elected head of the Mississippi NAACP.

1961

May: Twenty-seven Freedom Riders arrested in Jackson.

1962

Aug. 31:   Fannie Lou Hamer was part of a group that tried to register to
           vote in Sunflower County. She was asked to copy and interpret
           part of the Mississippi Constitution. She was able to copy it but
           unable to interpret it. On the way back home, the driver of the
           eighteen women was arrested for "driving a bus the wrong color."
           Later she was forced off the plantation and had to move from
           place to place. (Several Tutwiler Clinic employees knew her.)

Sept. 20: James Meredith tried to enroll at Ole Miss. Governor Ross Barnett
           denied it by standing in the door of the admissions office. The
           US Supreme Court ordered the university to allow him to attend
           classes. Riots ensued, leaving 175 injured, 212 arrested. Federal
           forces numbering 23,000 eventually were called out to keep
           order.

Dec. 4:   Fannie Lou Hamer returned to register to vote and passed the test.
           A US court order forced Mississippi to desegregate its state-run
           schools.

           Bob Tyler, a white coach at a Meridian high school, played a black
           student in a football game. The Klan burned a cross on his lawn.

1963

June 12:   Medgar Evers was shot and killed in his front yard in Jackson.
           A lawsuit was filed against WLBT-TV for refusing to sell Dr. Aaron
           Henry airtime during his gubernatorial bid. The station lost its
           license in 1969.

Aug. 18:   James Meredith became the first black to graduate from Ole Miss.
           Dr. Aaron Henry became president of COFO (Council of Federated
           Organizations), which planned the Freedom Summer in 1964.

1964

Feb. 14:   Whites abducted and whipped Alfred Whitley, a black employee at
           Armstrong Rubber Co. in Natchez.

Feb. 15:   Klansmen lured black mortician Archie Curtis and his assistant to a
           deserted field, stripped and beat them.

Feb. 28:   Clifford Walker, a black employee at International Paper Co. in
           Natchez, was killed on his way home. His car was found off

Highway 61, riddled with bullets, He was shot in the back. It was
the first killing identified by congressional investigators as the
work of the White Knights of the KKK. No one was prosecuted.

May 2:   Charles Moore and Henry Dee, students, both of Meadville, were
hitchhiking when two Klansmen passed by. They suspected the
two boys were involved in a rumored gun-smuggling operation
for an uprising by Black Muslims. The Klansmen went to get
help, abducted the boys, and drove [them] into Homochitto
National Forest, where they were tied to trees and beaten
unconscious. Later, a car drove into the woods, [and] the bodies
were lifted into the trunk, where a tarpaulin caught their blood.
They were taken to Louisiana, weighted down with a Jeep
motor block, and dumped in the Old River south of Tallulah.
Klansmen James Seale and Charles Edwards, employees of
International Paper Co. in Natchez, were arrested but never
tried.

June: James Meredith was shot on US Highway 51 near Hernando during
a voter registration march.

June 21: James Chaney, Andrew Goodman, [and] Michael Schwerner were
shot to death by Klansmen who had been ordered to do it by
Imperial Wizard Sam Bowers. They were buried in a levee
in Neshoba County. A jury convicted Bowers and six other
Klansmen of federal conspiracy charges, but no murder charges
were ever filed.

Aug.:   The Democratic National Convention was interrupted by the
Mississippi Freedom Democratic Party, which was led by Fannie
Lou Hamer. It demanded the seats of the regular Mississippi
delegation on grounds that half of the would-be electorate had
been denied [the] vote in violation of the Constitution. The
Credentials Committee of the Democratic Party seated the all-
white Mississippi delegation and two members of the integrated
Freedom Democratic Party.

Sept.:   The KKK bombed the home and later the grocery store of Mayor
John Nosser. The Klan bombed the home of Leonard Russell, a
black union worker.
James Winston, a black employee of International Paper Co., was
abducted and beaten.
Children of Lee Collins and Henrietta Franklin were among the
first to integrate the Marks public school system.

James Figgs was a student at MS Valley State when he acted as part
of the security team to ensure the safety of the families housing
Freedom Riders. He later took part in the mule train to DC.
Helen Ingram, age sixteen, and other students were attacked
and beaten unconscious for protesting the jailing of voter
registration workers.

Aug. 27:   George Metcalfe, president of the Natchez branch of the NAACP
and an employee at Armstrong Rubber Co., was nearly killed
when a bomb exploded in his car.

In 1964 alone in Mississippi there were eighty beatings, thirty-five
shootings, [and] sixty-eight bombings or burnings of churches,
businesses, and homes, much of it due to the White Knights of
the KKK.

1965

Aug. 15: Earl Hodges was beaten to death at his home after he reportedly tried
to leave the Klan. No one was ever prosecuted.

1966

Jan. 10:   Vernon Dahmer was an NAACP leader who was killed by the
White Knights of the Ku Klux Klan when his home and store
were firebombed just north of Hattiesburg. One Klansman
quoted Imperial Wizard Bowers as saying, "A jury would never
convict a white man for killin a nigger in Mississippi." Three
Klansmen were sentenced to life, but Bowers was freed after
mistrials resulted from hung juries.

June 10:   Three Klansmen—James Jones, Claude Fuller, and Ernest Avants—
lured Ben C. White to a secluded area of Natchez, where he was
killed. None of them was ever convicted. Later, testimony revealed
that they had hoped to lure Dr. Martin Luther King to Natchez.

Sept.:   Diane Hardy became the first black woman to be accepted into
Mississippi's only all-white women's college. Her family had
threatening phone calls, vandalism by the KKK. Her father
received numerous letters warning him that his job at Kerr-
McGee was in danger. She left after one year, returning in May
1992 to finish. She graduated in 1996.

Nov. 19:   A Natchez jewelry store was firebombed.
The home of an Adams County Supervisor was hit with a grenade.

1967

Feb. 27:   Wharlest Jackson, an employee of Armstrong Rubber Co., was
           killed on the way home when a time-delayed bomb blew up his
           pickup. Jackson had been offered and had accepted a promotion
           to a position historically held by white employees. The company
           was a center for White Knights of the KKK. No one was
           prosecuted. (See 1998.)

           Robert Clark was the first black since Reconstruction elected to the
           state House of Representatives.

May 12:   Ben Brown died after being struck by low officers' bullets in a
           demonstration on Lynch St. in Jackson. No one was ever
           prosecuted. Eyewitness accounts say he was struck in the back
           and base of the neck after leaving a store with a sandwich and a
           bottle of soda.

           Unita Blackwell became the first black woman mayor in Mississippi
           as mayor of Mayersville.

1968

Apr. 4:   Dr. Martin Luther King assassinated in Memphis at the Lorraine
           Motel

May 13:   Seventeen mule-drawn wagons filled with men, women, and
           children from Quitman County left Marks. It took thirty days to
           get to Atlanta, where they boarded a train [for] Washington, DC.
           The Poor People's March had been organized by Dr. King.

           JW Milam, one of the men who killed Emmett Till in 1955, died.

           State Representative Robert Clark introduced an education reform
           bill in the state legislature, requiring all children to attend
           school. (See 1982 and 2001.)

           Rainey Pool, a one-armed sharecropper, was beaten to death
           outside a bar and thrown off the bridge in Sharkey County into
           the Sunflower River. Judge B. B. Wilkes threw out Joe Watson's
           statement to the police in which he implicated himself and
           four others. Three days later, at the request of District Attorney
           George Everett, the charges were dismissed.

1970

May: Two students were killed by officers in a major racial disturbance at
           Jackson State University.

           Dr. Gilbert Mason was the first African American to be admitted to
           the Mississippi Academy of Family Physicians. (See 1959.)

1971

May: Jo Etha Collier was killed in a drive-by shooting in Drew. Three
         whites were charged.

1973

Gov. Bill Waller vetoed funding for the State Sovereignty
Commission.

1975

William Ayers filed a lawsuit against Mississippi because of the
segregated college system, which used standardized admissions
tests that discriminated against blacks. The case was settled in
1992.

1977

The Mississippi State Sovereignty Commission, a domestic spy
agency, was disbanded after waging a twenty-one-year war on
the civil rights movement. The state legislature sealed its records
for fifty years.

The Tuskegee Syphilis Study ended after forty years. The US
Public Health Service in Macon Co., Alabama, tracked the
natural history of untreated syphilis in 399 impoverished
black men, 274 of whom died. The men were never told
they had syphilis. The comprehensive summary was never
published, but thirteen articles later appeared in various
medical journals.

Eddie Carthan was elected the first black mayor of Tchula since
Reconstruction.

1980

Dr. Aaron Henry, a civil rights activist from Clarksdale, was elected
to the state legislature.

1982

The Education Reform Act was passed by the Mississippi state
legislature. Representative Robert Clark introduced it, and
it was only when William Winter became governor that it
passed, after fourteen years in the education committee of the
state legislature. This Act was the nation's first comprehensive
education reform, which established public kindergarten for all

Mississippi children, a minimum drop-out age, and mandatory attendance at school.

1983

Aug. 15:   The Tutwiler Clinic opened for patient care, following renovations in which the black waiting room was closed.

Oct.:   On the Friday before the dedication of the Clinic [. . .], the town clerk collected cookies from those who cared to bring them by city hall; she carefully gave Dr. Brooks two bags of store-bought cookies: "This one is from us and this one from the Nigras."

Standing at the checkout counter at Tutwiler Grain Elevator, one could see in the office a noose hanging from the wall with other memorabilia. It was not removed until 1996, when new owners took over.

1984

The Tutwiler Clinic hosted the Harvard School of Public Health Committee on Hunger in America as they evaluated the food stamp program at the twenty-year anniversary.

Opening of the black museum in Jackson as the Smith Robertson Museum and Cultural Center

The Confederate flag was officially dissociated with Ole Miss but continued to be waved at games.

There was a patient who came to the Tutwiler Clinic with bad arthritic pain, which had soured her disposition. On her second visit, scheduled to see if the arthritis medicine helped, she came in smiling, and said to Dr. Brooks, "Even if you are white, I'm gonna hug your neck." (Clarksdale *Press Register*)

1985

Legal action by the NAACP resulted in the division of the Town of Tutwiler into racially balanced voting wards that were approved by the Justice Department. Elections were supervised by federal poll watchers for several years after that.

July: Dr. Brooks was delegate and presenter at the Holy Names Justice Colloquium (Portland, OR).

1986

Indianola black residents boycotted schools and businesses in a predominantly (93 percent) black school district when a white

superintendent, W. A. Grissom, was appointed. Schools closed
for three weeks. White businessmen offered to buy his three-
year contract (his annual salary was $45,000), but he declined
the offer. A march held through the town was peaceful. The
only whites in the march were a priest and two nuns. Several
businesses closed permanently after a month of the boycott.
The Tutwiler Clinic Outreach Department received a grant for
workshops in child sexual abuse prevention. They were refused
the use of the meeting room at the Tutwiler Library, in spite of
appeals to the county.
In the Mississippi House of Representatives, eighteen black
members staged a three-day protest over the failure to pass the
bill making Dr. King's birthday a holiday. (Note that 15 January is
Robert E. Lee's birthday.)
Mike Espy was elected the first black member of the US Congress
since Reconstruction. He served seven years representing the
Second Congressional District, which comprised all or part of
twenty-four rural counties, including Tallahatchie.

1987

There was the town clean-up organized by Sister Maureen and the
Tutwiler Improvement Association, complete with the high
school band, trophies for the people who threw out the most
trash, certificates for the trashmen (who couldn't read them);
a flatbed was covered with funeral grass; speeches were made
by the mayor, the fire chief, the police chief, the doctor. The
townspeople came together, seemed to enjoy themselves, and
mixed without incident.
There were the efforts by the Tutwiler Improvement Association to
upgrade the debilitated phone system. The only building offered
for public meeting was one of the black churches in town, where
some white people did join blacks to work together on the
problem.

Apr.:   US district court Judge William Barbour ruled that eight of the
state's judicial districts violated Section 2 of the Voting Rights
Act of 1965.
Jimmie Holman became Marks's first black mayor under the newly
adopted ward system.

Aug.:   The white sheriff lost the election to Andrew Thompson, the first
black in Coahoma county to attain that office.

The first black woman to be elected to the state senate: Alice
Harden.

The Tutwiler Clinic hosted the US House of Representatives
Select Committee on Hunger and Infant Mortality, headed by
Congressman Mickey Leland, and including Congressman
Mike Espy. Dr. Brooks testified at the congressional hearing,
and escorted the members to visit Pearlie Taylor, a clinic patient
living in the plantation field hands' quarters, who opened her
"house" to the delegation. While they were there, the owner (also
a clinic patient) drove by several times in his pickup with his
rifle on the gun rack in back.

1988

Aug.:   Mayor of Glendora Johnny B. Thomas was found guilty of three
alcohol-related charges: possession for resale of seventy-two
bottles of whiskey, selling whiskey to a minor, selling beer to
a minor. He was sentenced to six months in jail with three
suspended and fined $1,700 plus court costs. He was acquitted
of four other charges: possession of less than an ounce of
marijuana, possession of paraphernalia, sale of whiskey after
hours, and sale of beer to a minor. The Mississippi Judicial
Performance Commission charged that he could not serve as
mayor and simultaneously as municipal judge. He was also
charged with accepting bribes and kickbacks in exchange for
allowing slot machines to operate in his town, which resulted in
an additional indictment on one count of conspiracy to obstruct
the criminal laws of M.

Fire destroyed the first black fraternity house on Ole Miss campus.
Ruled arson.

There was the effort by the Tutwiler Improvement Association (with
Sister Maureen behind the scenes) to get the down-river areas
dredged to prevent frequent flooding of the bayou in town.
Finally one day the secretary of the army and her entourage
drove into town for a meeting. The Methodist church had
graciously offered their Sunday school classroom as a meeting
place and served lunch to local and visiting dignitaries. It was
said later that one of the few families in that church refused to
continue their membership because blacks had been in their
building to a meeting.

1989

There was the time at white Easter sunrise service in Tutwiler where the Presbyterian minister (who happened to be a patient) suggested that the traditional collection be donated to the Clinic for all the good works done there instead of just put into a fund. There was no collection that year.

The White Citizens' Council closed. This organization was founded in the wake of *Brown vs. Board of Education* and led the battle to preserve segregation and the southern "way of life." Ross Barnett was their candidate for governor in the 1960s.

June: For the first time in Tutwiler history, the town board of aldermen had a 4–1 black majority (and four of the five were women).

Mayor Johnny B. Thomas of Glendora was sentenced to eight months in federal prison and five years' probation when he pleaded guilty to gambling charges (operating slot machines out of his cafe and getting bribes from the owners). He refused to step down as mayor even after he was sentenced.

Dr. Brooks testified before the Lower Mississippi Delta Commission, a congressional committee charged with finding ways to correct the fact that the country's poorest people lived on the richest land.

July: US District Court Judge William Barbour ruled that the records of the Sovereignty Commission sealed by the state legislature in 1977 should be opened; however, appeals by privacy advocate Rev. Ed King of Jackson kept the files sealed until 1998.

Aug.:   Dr. Brooks was a guest presenter at the United Auto Workers Civil Rights Seminar in Black Lake, Michigan.

1990

$476,000 in funds designated for Tallahatchie County were frozen because the supervisors did not comply with the unit system law passed in 1988.

Town of Tutwiler voting ward lines were redrawn after the census was completed.

There was the time after the airing of *60 Minutes* when the Baptist church in Tutwiler showed the videotape and had a discussion that went on into the night. Finally, after three weeks of silence, our neighbor, one of the deacons, came and told us he agreed with what we were doing and would side with us.

Twenty-two of the 122 state representatives and two of the state's fifty-two senators were black.

1991

The KKK paper "The World Wide Voice of the Aryan People" was left on Dr. Brooks's car. There was a note pasted on it: "WERE [sic] AWARE OF YOUR POLICY 'TO ONLY HELP BLACKS' NEVER WHITES UNLESS THEY WHORE WITH BLACK MEN. MAY GOD HAVE MERCY ON YOUR SOULS. FOR THE THOUSANDS OF DOLLARS AND DONATIONS YOU HAVE BEGGED OFF THE WHITE RACE."

Apr.: The US Dept of Justice rejected Tallahatchie Co redistricting plan for the Board of Supervisors because it was "legally unenforceable" due to components which inhibited black voters from electing candidates of their choice.

May 17: Tougaloo College, traditionally a black college, and a center for state civil rights activities, presented the Meritorious Leadership Award to Dr. Brooks.

July 29: A cross was burned and graffiti saying "KKK stay away" was on the window of a black family that planned to move into a white neighborhood in Grenada.

Aug. 4: An employer who hired black workers had a cross burned outside his home in northeastern Lowndes County near Columbus.

Dec.: The United Parcel Service provided a $100,000 grant to five families in Dirty Corner for rebuilding their homes. Jack Kemp, Secretary of Housing, and Mike Espy, District 2 Congressman, came for the ceremony.

1992

May 3: Two white men burned a cross on the yard of a black couple in the white Eupora community in DeSoto County. Each received six months to two years in prison.

June: The US Supreme Court in settlement of the Ayers case ruled that the state wipe out remnants of segregation at its eight universities.

Oct.: The College Board voted 8–4 for a desegregation plan to close traditionally black MS Valley State and merge traditionally black Alcorn State with other institutions. A flurry of legal activity followed to preserve their black identity but allow more white students to attend.

Dec.:   President Clinton named Mississippi Second District congressman
              Mike Espy to be Secretary of Agriculture.

1993

Jan. 22:   Six Kappa Sigma fraternity members from Ole Miss were in
              Charlottesville, Virginia, where they had gone to visit the
              national headquarters of their fraternity. Later they went to
              Crazy Charlie's Bar and Grill. They were becoming rowdy and
              refused to pay for their drinks. They were asked [to] leave the
              premises. The ensuing confrontation resulted not only in loud
              racial slurs, but Howard Weinberger, the manager, who was a
              black UVA student, was punched and kicked. The fraternity was
              suspended by Ole Miss.

Mar.:   The Commission on Human Rights Abuses in Mississippi met to
              examine black inmate deaths. The charges: "Since January 1990,
              more than 24 young African-American males have been arrested
              by various white law-enforcement officials on minor charges,
              and within hours of being in custody, these men have died. . . .
              Local law enforcement call their deaths 'suicide by hanging' but
              evidence indicates the hangings are in fact murders."

Mar.:   A West Clay High School teacher, Susan McBride, who taught
              biology and history, acknowledged she had referred to a messy
              desk in one of her classes as "nigger trash." The next day racial
              graffiti was sprayed on the school walls. The teacher was
              suspended, and school was dismissed for the rest of the week.

Apr.:   Opening of the National Civil Rights Museum in Memphis at the
              former Lorraine Motel.

Apr. 4:   Three white teens, Charles McGeehee, Roy McGovern, and Jerome
              Bellelo burned two black churches in Pike and Amite Counties.
              They pleaded guilty in US district court and were sentenced to
              three years in prison without parole.

May: The Justice Department began inspecting Mississippi county jails
              following complaints about jail suicides.

June: State and local NAACP chapters, the Legislative Black Caucus, and
              forty-nine individuals filed suit against Governor Fordice over
              the state flag, which contains the Confederate battle emblem.
              The case was again dismissed.

              Jerome Little and Bobbie Banks became the first blacks to be
              elected county supervisors from beats 4 and 5 respectively. Both
              are patients at the Clinic.

Luther Alexander, the first black admitted to the Delta Council, was
elected its vice president.

National Voter Registration Act passed, requiring states to make
registration forms available in driver's license bureaus, social
service agencies, and other state offices. The governor refused to
let it be in force in the state.

The Atlanta-based Heritage Preservation Association was founded
to "work to restore the civil rights of those who have been
discriminated against because of their Southern heritage." It
fought successfully to keep the Confederate flag flying over the
SC state capitol.

Mickey Thomas pleaded guilty to conspiracy to intimidate and
interfere with housing rights.

1994

Jan. 9:   Daniel Swan was convicted of burning a cross outside the home of
an interracial couple, Brenda and Earnest Polkey, in Improve in
Walthall County.

Jan.:   The Knights of the Ku Klux Klan paper announcing the National
Protest of Martin Luther King National Holiday was left on the
hood of Dr. Brooks's car.

Feb. 5:   Byron de la Beckwith was tried and convicted in the slaying of
Medgar Evers in 1963.

Sept. 11:   In New Augusta there was a noose found with a sign that said,
"Nigger, hang here."

Roy Bryant, one of the men who killed Emmett Till in 1955, died.

1995

Feb. 15:   Mississippi lawmakers finally ratified the US Constitution
amendment abolishing slavery.

May 21:   Three people were arrested in connection with the burning of
a cross outside the home of the Hooks family in the Helena
community north of Pascagoula. The black family had lived
there without incident for two years.

A flier was passed around Tutwiler by an irate black parent: "Learn
how Mayor Phil Jennings has physically assaulted one of our
children, stalked another of our children with a rifle, threatened
to kill these children, and used vulgar and abusive language to
the mother and grandmother in the family."

1996

At the Democratic National Convention in Chicago, Senator Johnnie Walls honored Emmett Till's mother, Mrs. Mamie Till Mobley.

Apr.: The KKK held a rally in Tupelo but refused to pay the $50 fee. Legal action ensued.

June: A federal appeals court ruled that the secret files of the state's defunct segregationist spy agency, the Mississippi Sovereignty Commission, be opened.

July: There was the dilapidated house next to the library that had been condemned by the town of Tutwiler. It was sold to a black contractor, who was fixing it up. It happened that across the street was the home of the owner of the white funeral home who couldn't bear "waking up in the morning and looking across the street at that n____." So he burned it down. The five plantation owners who had stock in the cotton gin that was behind the torched house paid off the contractor and turned the land into parking for the gin.

Dr. Brooks testified before the Mississippi Joint House and Senate Health Maintenance Organization Oversight Committee in Jackson regarding the effect of HMOs on Medicaid patients.

Sept.: Governor Fordice nominated four white men to the state College Board. The names were rejected by the state senate committee. He resubmitted the same names. Then he tried to appoint them by saying that there was pressing College Board business and there was no legal quorum.

Nov.: Robert Grayson became the first black mayor of Tutwiler.

1997

Jan.: Medgar Evers's brother Charles, age seventy-five, published a biography of his brother.

Jan. 30: Ole Miss "Miss University" Pageant had two contenders, one black and one white. They had tied in overall competitions. The rules stated that the one who scored highest in talent wins the overall title. There was a five-way tie in talent that included both women. An independent auditor decreed that the tie should have been resolved using the outcome of the interview section. In the end, the wrongly named first winner, Anne Crowson, was allowed to keep her $1,100 scholarship, and an additional one was given to Carissa Wells, the actual winner, who was black.

Feb.:   The Martin Luther King Jr. Award was presented to Dr. Brooks by
            the International Fellowship of Reconciliation.
May 19:   Aaron Henry died in Clarksdale. A civil rights activist, Dr. Henry
            was head of the NAACP in the 1960s [and] served in the
            Mississippi House of Representatives from 1980 to 1996. In the
            '60s his house was firebombed twice, and his pharmacy once.
            The pharmacy was a local civil rights memorial when it was
            burned in 1993.
Oct. 22:   Ole Miss limited the size of Confederate flags allowed at games and
            became the ninth Southeastern Conference school to ban sticks
            from its stadium.
Nov. 18:   White supremacist and Rankin County attorney Richard Barrett
            sued Ole Miss University over banning the Confederate flag.
            He claimed security officers forced him and two friends to
            take down a 3 ft x 5 ft rebel flag at the football stadium and
            threatened to arrest them during the game.
Nov. 24:   In a rally held in Oxford, the members of the League of the South
            (membership at 5,000) [and] the Council of Conservative
            Citizens (membership at 100,000) joined in public protest at the
            above event.
Nov. 25:   The Heritage Preservation Association opened a Mississippi
            chapter. (See 1993.)
            Gov. Fordice failed to stop the funding for the minority Business
            Loan Program. His veto was overridden.
            Black deckhands won a $1.2 million settlement from the US Army
            Corps of Engineers for enduring years of on-the-job racial
            harassment, in which they were repeatedly passed over for
            promotion and subjected to derogatory statements from white
            workers aboard the dredge *Hurley*. For sixty-four years no black
            workers were offered full-time jobs aboard Corps dredges in the
            Memphis district.
            There was a disturbance by three black students who ripped rebel
            flags off the walls in an Oxford barbeque.

1998

            The governor declared the "Motor Voter Law of 93" [...] an
            unconstitutional imposition on his state's rights. He demanded
            photo identification at each election. (Overruled by the state
            legislature.)

The City of Jackson was ordered to pay damages in a lawsuit when the council rejected a contractor's low bid. The city had a law that minority participation must get 15 percent of contracts, and the contractor did not have enough minority subcontractors listed in his bid.

Former Imperial Wizard of the KKK, Sam Bowers, was convicted of the death of Vernon Dahmer and sentenced to life in prison. (See 1966.)

The Tutwiler Community Education Center invited Mae Bertha Carter, the author of *Silver Rights* to speak at an evening gathering. She described her experiences of having her children be the first blacks to attend the public school in Sunflower County. At the refreshments afterwards, one of the white ladies in the audience approached Sister Joann, recounting how she had been the teacher of some of these children at this school, and how bad she had felt, seeing how cruelly the other children treated the newcomers, especially on the playground. The teacher recalled that she didn't know how to handle the problem. Shortly, Sister Joann introduced the guest to the former teacher of her children so she could bring to closure a difficult problem in their lives.

Jan: Civil rights activist and lawyer Cleve McDowell was shot dead by Juarez Webb, nineteen. His collection of civil rights papers went up in flames some months later when his law office burned. McDowell was the second black student to enroll in Ole Miss in 1963. He was later expelled from the university's law school after he was found carrying a concealed weapon.

James Farmer was awarded the Presidential Medal of Freedom for a lifetime of activism. He was in jail in Louisiana during the 1963 march on Washington; during the Nixon administration he was an assistant secretary in the Dept. of Health, Education, and Welfare. At the time of the award, he was teaching history at Mary Washington College in Fredericksburg, Virginia, even though he was a bilateral amputee and blind from diabetes.

Feb.:   Harrison County supervisors agreed to erect a monument and marker in honor of those who protested and eventually desegregated the beaches. (See 1959.)

A Starkville policeman walked around in the police department wearing an old KKK robe found in the evidence locker. He was

suspended without pay and served a six-month probation and
had to attend a community diversity training seminar.

Mar.:   Legislative Black Caucus members asked for the resignations
of Sam Polles, executive director of the state Department of
Wildlife, Fisheries and Parks, and his deputy administrator.
The allegations were that minorities had been relegated to
"demeaning jobs" and denied opportunities for advancement
in the department. There were thirteen African Americans out
of four hundred game wardens. The agency came under federal
review in January.

Mar. 17:   State Sovereignty Commission records (about 132,000 pages) were
finally opened. (See 1999.)

Aug.:   Second District US Rep. Bennie Thompson asked Defense Secretary
William Cohen to investigate charges that hundreds of African
American troops may have been slaughtered at Camp Van Dorn,
Mississippi, in 1943. Author Carroll Case, a former bank official
in McComb, charges that black members of the 364th Infantry
division were massacred. (This was later shown to be false.)
In Natchez, the attorney general's office began moving toward
re-prosecuting the murder of Wharlest Jackson. (See 1967.)

Marks: A weekend reenactment of the Mule Train ride from Marks to
Atlanta as part of the Poor Peoples' March on Washington was
held with many local residents who had participated in 1968.
Photos are displayed in the Civil Rights Museum in Atlanta
across from Ebenezer Baptist Church.
Jackson city officials pushed for the prosecution of the killer of Ben
Brown, a co-worker of Medgar Evers, shot as he left a store on
Lynch St. years ago. (See 1967.)
The district attorney reopened the case of Rainey Pool, a black man
who was beaten to death and tossed off the bridge in Sharkey
County in 1970. Charged with murder were Joe Watson, James
and Charles Caston, their half brother, Hall Crimm, and Dennis
Newton. Watson was not originally indicted, but new evidence
and inconsistencies resulted in reinvestigation. [, . .]
An employee of the Tutwiler Clinic had saved enough to buy a
house. She lived in Clarksdale, and had driven around to check
out neighborhoods she liked where houses had For Sale signs.
She contacted the real estate agent, who, over the course of a
couple of weeks, showed her several homes for sale. She never

went to the neighborhood where the employee wished to locate. When questioned about the house, the agent said someone had bought it; when the employee insisted on going by it with the agent, there was no SOLD sign up, and it was still listed. But it was in a white neighborhood. The employee purchased the house.

1999

Charles Noble, a Sanderson Farm executive, faced trial in connection with the slaying of NAACP leader Vernon Dahmer in 1966. It [was] the last trial remaining in the case; in 1998 former KKK Imperial Wizard Sam Bowers was convicted of murder and sentenced to life in prison. The third defendant, Deavours Nix, died in September 1998.

Jan.:   District Attorney of Philadelphia, Mississippi, reopened the case of the KKK killings of Michael Schwerner, Andrew Goodman, and James Chaney.

Mar.:   The members of the state Congressional Black Caucus introduced a resolution condemning the Council of Conservative Citizens as racist. This was in response to a speech made by Mississippi's US senator Trent Lott to the Council, and his subsequent efforts to distance himself from the group.

The Town of Tutwiler still did not have twenty-four-hour police coverage.

Mar.:   US district court Judge William Barbour resolved the privacy claims by forty-two people named in the Mississippi Sovereignty Commission. The list of whose files will be opened or closed remains unavailable, pending further appeals or the expiration of time for appeals.

May: A proposed leadership institute named for Senate Majority Leader Trent Lott of Mississippi has become the target of publicity because of the senator's links to the white supremacist group Council of Conservative Citizens. Large corporations are under fire for donating to the institute.

The Mississippi Supreme Court reinstated the lawsuit over the state flag, which had been thrown out in 1993 by a Hinds County judge. There was one black member of the state supreme court.

Black voters challenged the Mississippi Public Service Commission districts as discriminatory. The three existing districts have majority white populations and use the same boundaries as Supreme Court justice elections. Lawyers from Coahoma and Bolivar Counties are requesting a 55 percent majority black district that would run the length of the western side of the state.

June: The KKK staged a march in Canton (black majority population with its first black mayor). Only one hundred people showed up. No incidents occurred.

In the calling of prospective jurors for the upcoming trial of the murder of Vernon Dahmer (see 1966), it happened that his son was one of the residents of Forrest Co. whose names were pulled by a mathematical formula. Both sides agreed to allow him to be removed from the list.

Rosa Parks, 86, was honored with the Congressional Gold Medal. (See 1955.)

The trial of Charles Noble for the firebombing slaying of Vernon Dahmer was declared a mistrial when Bill Roy Pitts, who accused Noble, testified he felt threatened by Carl Ford, one of Sam Bowers's defense lawyers, when he encountered him two days ago in a restaurant. (Pitts is a former Klansman who had testified that Bowers ordered the slaying and had identified eight people, including Noble, who carried out the firebombing.)

On the thirty-fifth anniversary, dozens retraced the Freedom Riders' routes from 1964. Ben Chaney, brother of James, who had been murdered with Andrew Goodman and Mickey Schwerner and their bodies buried in a levee (see 1964), called for the state "to fulfill its judicial responsibility by prosecuting those who conspired and committed the murders."

The jury acquitted Dennis Howell Newton in the killing of Rainey Pool (see 1970), finding that he was a bystander. He is the first of five to go on trial for the murder.

Sept. 14: Alton Wayne Roberts died of heart failure at age sixty-one. The Klansman had been convicted of federal conspiracy charges in connection with the June 21, 1964 (qv) slaying of Michael Schwerner, Andrew Goodman, and James Chaney. Testimony said he had fatally shot Schwerner and Goodman; Chaney died of several gunshots. Efforts had been ongoing to retry him for murder.

Nov. 13: James "Doc" Caston, 66, of Satartia; his brother, Charles Caston, 64, of Holly Bluff; and their half-brother, Hal Crimm, 50, of

Vicksburg were convicted by a Humphreys County jury in the killing of Rainey Pool. (See 1970.) They were sentenced to twenty years. The fifth man, the state's key witness, John Watson, 57, of Rolling Fork, testified that he and the trio beat and kicked Pool. After Pool was knocked unconscious, Watson said, he and Crimm loaded Pool into his pickup and dumped Pool into the Sunflower River. Watson received four years for manslaughter. *Clarion Ledger* 18 Nov 99 p. 1.

Nov. 29:   A new investigation into the Ku Klux Klan's 1966 (qv) slaying of Ben Chester White is under way. Although the only living suspect, Ernest Avants of Bogue Chitto, was acquitted of murder and cannot be tried again for the same offense. However, it was discovered that the murder took place in the Homochitto National Forest, which comes under federal jurisdiction, thus permitting a retrial. (*Clarion Ledger* 29 Nov 99 p. 1A)

2000

Jan. 14:   A new investigation into the deaths of Henry Dee and Charles Moore (see 1964) may begin, since they also were killed by the Ku Klux Klan in the Homochitto National Forest, which is under the FBI rather than the state. Of the two who are alleged to have killed these men, only Charles Edwards is alive. State police reports claim he admitted he was involved in beating the two but maintained they were left alive. However, the files have been destroyed "in the ordinary course of business." Bill Dukes, a Gulfport lawyer who had investigated the case for the FBI, did not want to discuss it. (*C. Ledger* 14 Jan 00)

Jan. 18:   At his murder trial, prosecutors did not use Ernest Avants's admission to the FBI that he was involved in the killing of Ben Chester White (see 1966), and he was acquitted. Two other men were arrested: James Jones and Claude Fuller. Jones confessed but jurors deadlocked, and a mistrial was declared. Fuller was never tried. Prosecutors never called then–highway patrolman Donald Butler, who would have testified that Jones identified Avants and Fuller as taking part in White's killing; nor was Jones's confession introduced (he implicated Avants and Fuller). (*C. Ledger* 18 Jan 00)

June 8:   Ernest Avants, 68, was indicted on a federal murder charge thirty-four years after the Klan killed Ben Chester White (see 1966 and above Nov. 29 1999).

June 14:   The TV show *20/20* interviewed Ernest Gilbert, a Klansman turned
           FBI informant, regarding the deaths of Henry Dee and Charles
           Moore (see 1964 and Jan. 14 above). The evidence was presented
           to the district attorney Lenox Foreman of Meadville in 1965 by
           the FBI, but it was never presented to the grand jury. (*C. Ledger*
           14 Jun 00 1A)

July 31:   The State Dept. of Archives and History opened six thousand more
           pages of the Mississippi Sovereignty Commission (1956–1973),
           including some of Aaron Henry and Charles Evers. Judge Barbour
           ruled that heirs and kin of the dead cannot pursue a privacy claim.
           There are also 146 pages of rebuttals from people named in the
           records, and 1,800 pages remain sealed. (*C. Ledger* 31 Jul 00 1B)

Sept. 25: Dr. Gilbert Mason has published *Beaches, Blood and Ballots: A Black
           Doctor's Civil Rights Struggle* (see 1959, 1970). (Jackson *Clarion
           Ledger* 25 Sep 00 p. 1)

Dec. 15:   Charles Noble accused key prosecution witness Billy Roy Pitts
           of committing perjury and said he had been denied a speedy
           trial (seventeen months after a mistrial was declared in the
           firebombing death of Vernon Dahmer (qv 1966). Noble was
           indicted Jan. 24, 1968, on murder and arson charges but was not
           tried on the state charges. (*C. Ledger* 15 Dec., p. 1A)

2001

April: Jerry Sharpe, a suspect in the Schwerner, Goodman, and Chaney
           case from 1964 (qv), died before trial. The case had been
           reopened in 1999, and an informant had been located. There
           are other potential witnesses of the role of Edgar Ray Killen (a
           Klansman who had reportedly given orders on what to do that
           night) are: Ernest Gilbert, a Klansman-turned-FBI-informant
           who says three suspects implicated in the trio's killings took part
           in a similar Klan kidnapping of a black teen three weeks earlier,
           and Bob Stringer, who says he heard Sam Bowers (already
           convicted) give Killen the orders to kill Schwemer. Jackson, MS
           Clarion Ledger 3 May 2001 p. 4A.

April: A state referendum was held regarding replacing the state flag
           with its Confederate emblem. The vote was heavily in favor of
           retaining the flag.

May 2:   A majority white jury convicted former Klansman Thomas Blanton
           of murder in a 1963 bombing of the 16th St Baptist Church in

Atlanta in which 4 young girls were killed. Jackson, MS *Clarion Ledger* 2 May 01 p. 1A.

May: Hinds County grand jury concluded that two lawmen were responsible for the death of twenty-two-year-old Ben Brown, who was shot in the back 11 May 67 (qv) during a protest near the campus of Jackson State College.

June: Governor William Winter was awarded the Martin Luther King Jr. Memorial Award by the National Education Association for successfully leading the nation's first comprehensive education reform act of 1982 (qv). *Clarion Ledger*, 26 June 01 p. 1B.

Carol Ruth Silver, a sixty-two-year-old attorney from San Francisco, began organizing a reunion of the Freedom Riders in Jackson at Tougaloo College, November 8–11. The message is one of reconciliation, making a monument to the history of the civil rights movement and allowing kids in Mississippi to understand it. She has compiled a list of 416 former Freedom Riders by searching the Jackson police records and the archives of the *Clarion Ledger*.

[The list of Freedom Riders and related materials from the Civil Rights Movement Veterans website (crmvet.org) appear here in the original document.]

Dr. Celeste Cook-Glenn (pathologist) and Dr. Clyde Glenn (psychiatrist and pastor of a large Clarksdale Church) had applied to the Clarksdale Country Club for membership. Both are black. The three-member secret committee and the board of directors approved them, but the membership did not. John Faulkner, CEO of the hospital in Clarksdale, NW MS Regional Medical Center, invited the president and officers over for lunch, and the decision was made to change the bylaws to allow a simple majority of club members to vote no to reject an applicant, and to remove the requirement that if only twenty-five of the members present vote against admission, the person cannot become a member.

July 16:   At the country club meeting to ratify the bylaws change, of the 402 voting members, 192 were present, and more than 130 voted to reject the bylaw change. Subsequently a letter condemning the conduct of Mr. Faulkner and requesting his removal as CEO was sent to the president of Health Management Associates, his employer. This letter was forwarded to the regional vice president, Joe Mullaney, who tore it up. One of the other staff physicians stated it was not a racial thing but the ability to control the membership. But he went on to say he was going to boycott the new restaurant in town partly owned by one of the club members who introduced the bylaw change. This same physician has voiced complaints about the work done by the pathologist on several occasions since her inclusion on the staff of the hospital.

July 21:   The Clarksdale *Press Register* carried a front-page article reporting disagreement among the Clarksdale Country Club members about the proper parliamentary procedure and whether the vote was valid.

July 26:   The Jackson *Clarion Ledger* printed an editorial condemning the action (p. 6a).

Sept.:   The Clarksdale *Press Register* reported that the wife and widow of Ben Brown (see 1967) [. . .] filed a $20 million lawsuit against the estates of his two alleged assailants, the city of Jackson and the state Dept of Public Safety. Clarksdale *Press Register* 31 Oct 01 p. 2A.

2002

Jan.:   The three-judge panel of the 5th US Circuit Court of Appeals unanimously reinstated an incriminating statement by Ernest Avants, charged in the KKK 1966 killing of farmhand Ben Chester White (see 1966). This would be the first federal trial in a civil rights era killing. Avants is the only remaining suspect in that case. (Had heart surgery 7 Feb 02.) Jackson *Clarion Ledger* 9 Jan 02 p. 1A.

Feb. 15   Judge Biggers signed off on a $503 million settlement plan to end the twenty-seven-year desegregation battle. Senate voted 33–10, House 100–20. About $300M in funding could be held up if the ruling is appealed. The plan includes $245M for academic programs at the three historically black universities, $75M for facilities and $83M already spent on Ayers. Jackson *Clarion Ledger* 18 Feb 02 p.1A.

May 24:   Mississippi Supreme Court upheld the convictions of James Caston, Hal Crimm (sentenced in 1999 to 20 years for manslaughter in the case of Rainey Pool). The argument had been that they were both represented by the same lawyer. (See 1970). Jackson *Clarion Ledger* 24 May 02 p. 1B.

June 12:   Written in black spray paint on the street in front of the Barnards'
            house in Tutwiler: "All you KKK must die!" Someone took white
            spray paint, put xxx through KKK and wrote "niggers."
Dec.:   Mississippi senator Trent Lott, after making remarks at Sen. Strom
            Thurmond's 100th birthday party, resigned from his position as
            majority leader of the US Senate.

2003

Jan. 9:   Belle Davidson, the first person to find Ben Chester White's bullet-
            riddled body (on June 10, 1966 [qv]) died. She was to have been
            a witness in the trial of Ernest Avants. She is the one who would
            testify that the body was found in the Homochitto National
            Forest, which is federal land, making federal prosecution
            possible. The defendant had been acquitted of the state murder
            charge. Jackson *Clarion Ledger* 1 Jan 03 p. 1A

Jan 24:   Ernest Avants, age seventy-one, was ruled competent to stand trial
            for the KKK killing of Ben Chester White in 1966 (qv) *Clarion
            Ledger* 24 Jan 03.

June 18:   Ernest Avants was given life sentence in the killing of Ben Chester
            White in 1996 (qv) Jackson *Clarion Ledger* 18 Jun 03 p. 1A.

Oct. 15:   Jackson City Council settled a $20 million wrongful death suit
            brought by the family of civil rights activist Ben Brown (qv),
            who was shot to death on his twenty-second birthday as he
            walked to a restaurant during a riot at Jackson State College in
            1967. Jackson *Clarion Ledger* Oct 15, 2003 p. 1A.

Nov. 4:   Appeal of the Ayers case settlement opened in the 5th US Circuit
            Court of Appeals. The settlement includes $246 million for
            academic programs, $75 million for facilities, $70 million
            public endowment, $35 million private endowment, and money
            for summer programs for students who don't meet regular
            admission standards. Universities must reach at least 10 percent
            nonblack enrollment before they can get full access to the
            endowments. The original agreement settlement was signed
            by US District Judge Neal Biggers in Feb 2002 after the state
            legislature agreed to fulfill it. Jackson *Clarion Ledger* Nov 4 2003
            p. 1B.

2004

Feb. 5:   Panel heard an appeal in Ernest Avants's case; they threw out the
            federal murder conviction, because the defense should have

been allowed to introduce more evidence to discredit James
Jones (now deceased), whose statement implicated Avants in the
murder of black handyman Ben Chester White. (See 1966.) After
White's killing, Jones confessed and was arrested with Avants
and Claude Fuller. Jones expressed remorse, and a hung jury
led to a mistrial. Avants was acquitted in a 1967 trial. The ruling
[would] be made later. Jackson *Clarion Ledger* Feb 5 2004 p. 1B.

May 11:   The Justice Dept. reopened the investigation into the 1955 murder of
Emmett Till (qv).

May 20:   Ayers case appeal going to Supreme Court. Alvin Chambliss
of Oxford, lead attorney for private plaintiffs trying to opt
out of a proposed settlement in the case, argued that a $503
million settlement was reached under Fourteenth Amendment
guidelines, but it should have been based on the Title VI criteria
in the Civil Rights Act of 1964. Proposed settlement called for
$246 million to be spent over seventeen years on academic
programs at JSU, Alcorn, and Valley to attract white students;
$75 million for capital improvements, $70 million to public
endowments, and $35 million in private endowments. Other
programs would receive the balance. Jackson *Clarion Ledger* 20
May 04 p. B1.

June 14: Ernest Avants died in prison in Jackson, Mississippi, of
complications from heart problems.

July: The Mississippi delegation to the Democratic Convention was
seated and included one member from the original [delegation].

Sept. 20: Key suspect in Klan's 1964 killings of Chaney, Goodman, and
Schwerner (qv) Edgar Ray Killen (age seventy-nine) supposedly
agreed to make an appearance at the Neshoba County Fair
booth for the white supremacist organization known as the
Nationalist Movement. This was headed by lawyer Richard
Barrett. However, Killen denied he had ever agreed, and the
booth was cancelled. Jackson, MS, *Clarion Ledger* 20 Sep 04 p.
1A.

Oct. 18: The US Supreme Court refused to hear an appeal on the Ayers
case, ending Mississippi's nearly thirty-year-old legal battle
over higher education desegregation. The funding is a major
problem, with $22.56 million not funded since 2002. Jackson
Clarion Ledger 10 Oct 04 p. 1A.

Nov.:   An appeal of the $503M Ayers settlement agreement. Would
benefit Jackson State University, Alcorn, and Mississippi Valley

Universities. The settlement was signed by US District Judge
Neal Biggers Jr. in Feb '02. Attorney Chambliss stated the
agreement is "unconstitutional, unfair and unreasonable because
of governance, mission and funding formula issues. Missions do
not include law and pharmacy. Admission standards keep some
black students from attending college and should be lowered.
First-time freshmen dropped from >300 in 1975 to about 1,500
in 1999 (18.4 percent in '94 to 13.2 percent in '98). Percentage of
black students enrolled in predominantly white universities 10.7
percent in '94 and 12.1percent in '98.

Dec. 21:   The Jackson City Council voted to add Medgar Evers's surname to
the Jackson International Airport.

2005

Jan. 7:   The grand jury indicted Edgar Ray Killen in slayings of Michael
Schwerner, James Chaney, and Andrew Goodman (qv). Killen
was arrested at his home in Jackson 6 Jan. He was seventy-nine.
He pleaded not guilty. He was held without bond originally, then
bond was set for $250,000. He was released from the Neshoba
County jail on Jan. 13. The trial was set for March. Jackson
Clarion Ledger Jan 05, 6–13.

Feb. 25:   JJ Harper of Cordele, Georgia, Imperial Wizard of the American
White Knights of the Ku Klux Klan, requested permission to
demonstrate on the lawn of the Neshoba County courthouse in
support of Killen. Jackson *Clarion Ledger* Feb 25, 2004 p. 1B.

May 17:   Transcript of first Till trial found. One of the suspects was Carolyn
Bryant, wife of Roy Bryant, who was tried and acquitted in 1955.

June 2:   Investigators exhumed Emmett Till's (qv 1955) body in preparation
for [the] trial. No autopsy was ever performed prior to burial in
Chicago.

June 10:   Efforts were made to postpone the trial of Edgar Ray Killen, age
eighty, at the Neshoba County courthouse. The judge declined.

June 14:   Trial of KKK leader Killen began; ended with a verdict of guilty of
manslaughter, sentenced to twenty years.

July 1:   Highway 49 E between Tutwiler and Greenwood dedicated to the
memory of Emmett Till. Ceremonies were held at each end
of the designated road, with family members from Chicago in
attendance.

July 23:   A lawyer in Kentucky had a client who admitted he bought two
guns in the late '60s from Neshoba Co sheriff Lawrence Rainey,

now deceased. (Rainey had been acquitted in a 1967 federal conspiracy case.) The guns were turned over for testing.

Nov. 23: The FBI probe into the 1955 killing of Emmett Till was officially concluded.

Dec. 9: Henry Kirksey died of pneumonia. Was a plaintiff, expert witness, and community organizer whose effort led to the election of almost six hundred African Americans to public office in Mississippi. Jackson *Clarion Ledger* p. lA.

2006

Jan. 15: Call from William Matthews . . . whose father served on the jury in the trial for Emmett Till's murderers. He wanted to talk to Woodrow (Champ) Jackson, who had embalmed Emmett's body, to ask him about an unidentified body found at the same time, so as to exonerate his father and clear his name for his part as a juror. No further contact with Mr. Jackson, due to his health.

Apr. 28: Bill was introduced in the US Congress to create a cold cases unit in the Justice Dept. dedicated to the investigation of unpunished killings of the civil rights era. Jackson *Clarion Ledger* 28 Apr 06 p. 1B.

May 18: Clyde Kennard cleared after forty-six years (an army sergeant wrongly imprisoned for burglary in 1960 after refusing to abandon his quest to enroll at a local all-white university). This followed a three-month investigation by the Jackson *Clarion Ledger* into his innocence. He died of colon cancer shortly after his release from prison in 1963.

Nov. 5: Sam Bowers, former Imperial Wizard of the KKK, died at Mississippi State Penitentiary at Parchman. He was eighty-two. His remains were claimed by an out-of-state family member. Jackson *Clarion Ledger* 6 Nov 06, p. 1A.

Nov. 14: A review team in the Till case is expected to meet in December, and if it thinks the case should go forward, it most likely would go to a grand jury from LeFlore County. Jackson *Clarion Ledger* 14 Nov 06 p. 1A.

2007

Jan.: James Ford Seale of Roxie pleaded not guilty to federal kidnapping and conspiracy charges in connection with the May 2, 1964, abduction, beatings, and drownings of Henry Dee and Charles Moore (qv). Jackson *Clarion Ledger* Feb 28, 2007 p. 1B.

Feb. 27:   Grand jury in Leflore County did not indict anyone in the 1955
           killing of Emmett Till. Jackson *Clarion Ledger* Feb 27, 2007 p. lA.
Aug. 25:   Judge Henry Wingate gave maximum sentence of three life terms
           to James Seale for the deaths of Henry Dee and Charles Moore
           (qv). Jackson *Clarion Ledger* 25 Aug.
Oct. 2:   A state historical marker identifying the site of the 1955 trial of
           two men charged with the murder of Emmett Till (qv) was
           dedicated at the Tallahatchie County courthouse in Sumner in
           a public ceremony. A resolution [...] drafted by the Emmett
           Till Memorial Commission, with the assistance of staff at the
           William Winter Institute for Racial Reconciliation at Ole Miss
           [would] be read and published. (See 1955.) Tallahatchie Co. *Sun
           Sentinel*, p. 1.
Oct. 9:   Rev. William Milam, the grandson of one of the men charged and
           acquitted in that killing, accepted the pastorship of the Sumner
           Baptist Church. He was welcomed by the various pastors and
           members of their church communities and asked to preach at
           the ecumenical service at Thanksgiving.

2008

           The Clarksdale Country Club admitted Dr. Ken Kellough, MD, an
           African American and a local doctor.

Appendix 5

THE ANNUAL ANDREW TAYLOR STILL MEMORIAL ADDRESS

Dr. Brooks delivered this address July 17, 1993, at the American Osteopathic Association convention in Chicago, Illinois.

Presenting this address is an opportunity for me to step out of the isolation of the Mississippi Delta with its local problems and to take a national, even a global, view of our profession. I want to look behind and before, and I want to speak of the reality of osteopathic medicine as the twenty-first century approaches. . . . Andrew Taylor Still was only too aware of the inadequacies of medical practice in his century. It challenged him enough that he became determined to look at medicine from a radically different angle. That he succeeded has been proven by the existence of our profession. We have proudly counted our first one hundred years of service, during which the profession made enormous strides as it grew from a tiny group in the middle of our country to one of international stature.

Dr. Still was a man who assessed his talents. He learned who he really was, and he acted on that knowledge to improve life for others. This is our mandate as our second hundred years begins. We must take an "A. T. Still view" of the challenges and inadequacies of the medical practice of our day by looking at medicine from a radically different angle. I am challenging you to accept responsibility for change. That is a tough request because most of the time, we do not want to change. . . . . As osteopathic physicians living at the end of the twentieth century, we are well equipped to follow in Dr. Still's footsteps. And we are again challenged to make a radical difference in the health of humanity. . . .

RADICAL means taking away the pedestals on which physicians stand.

RADICAL means reforming the legal system.

RADICAL means making healthcare available to all, bringing justice and speed to reimbursement, and ending hassles with third-party payers.

RADICAL means keeping patients in good health and lowering costs.

Being radical is tough if you are doing it alone. We need to enable others to join us in this effort. To meet this challenge, we have to educate our patients because we empower them when we do so. . . . The motto of osteopathic medicine in the twenty-first century should be Educate to Empower for Health. Education then becomes preventive medicine at its best, and we become prevention specialists. Prevention specialists are primary educators. . . . As physicians, we have years and years of study and knowledge behind us. And most of the time, our patients have come to respect that knowledge. . . . .

We have the power to educate for health in a proactive fashion. Before the cancer starts, before age breaks down bony structures, before plaque invades arteries, before the teen-ager becomes pregnant, and before stress gets the upper hand, we must be there with knowledge and time to educate patients to prevent problems. That would truly lower healthcare costs. . . . . We must teach our patients to become part of the healthcare team and bear responsibility for their actions. We don't heal: Patients have the capacity to heal themselves. What they need is direction, a gentle touch and treatment.

We are the facilitators, not the healers. Physicians need to: Really listen to catch potential problems,

- Be straightforward in explanations, for example, use "hand-scribbled stick figures to explain the transmission of venereal disease"
- Educate the patient when and how to use the emergency room
- Take advantage of generic drugs
- Involve the patient in your decisions
- Educate patients about the destructive nature of stress
- Realize how "consumerism fractionates families"
- Practice positive thinking, laughter, compliments and good news "to help lance the gloom and doom that so easily builds into stress"
- Involve the family—as early as possible, "have upfront, honest discussions with the family away from the terrifying hospital setting" about your prognosis and recommendations—Death is a scary business.

And lastly realize that our own lives also require preventive medicine. We must do the hardest thing in the world and look honestly at what our lifestyles are doing to ourselves and our families, friends and colleagues. If our stress levels have turned us into monsters whom others avoid, or if we have become so exhausted that we have turned into stone walls that block communication, we need to look this problem squarely in the eye and have the courage to hear what family members and friends are trying to tell us.

Our own little ruts can feel pretty safe. But sameness can become monotony. That can lead to depression, which has the potential for turning our ruts into our graves. So we must be willing to apply an A. T. Still approach to ourselves and dare to be radically different. Now, let's shift gears into forward. Who is the DO of the future? In the future, we should be:

- Radical and creative thinkers and proactive educators for ourselves and our patients.
- Come off our pedestals and become listeners: compassionate, holistic healers, and prevention specialists.
- Empower our patients for health so that they can join us in our efforts to change our healthcare system for the better. We can't do it alone.

The future is one in which every patient is important and in which every ounce of prevention is worth a pound of cure. This vision of the future begins now, and to be successful we need enthusiasm and new energy.

WORKS CONSULTED

Newspapers, Periodicals, and Reports

ACGP Newsletter, vol. 9, no. 10, December 1992

American Health, "Healing the Delta" by Frank Clancy, November 1990

Baxter Allegiance Foundation, Annual Report, 1998

Caring, People, vol. 5, Winter 1992

Catholic Key, December 6, 2002

Catholic Register, December 2002

Catholic Review, March 13, 2003

Catholic Sentinel, January 2003, September 1994

Chicago Tribune, March 29, 1931

Christopher News Notes, no. 334

Clarion Ledger, 3/17/86, 10/17/93, 7/22/97, 8/16/98

Clarksdale Press Register, 9/20/95, 2/14/96, 4/2/97, 2/27/98, 10/16/98, 9/10/99, 2/16/00, 4/27/27/00, 3/22/03,6/7/03,11/27/04, 3/24/05, 11/15/05

Clinical Advisor, May 1999

Clockworks, The Reading Hospital and Medical Center, vol. 1, Now April 1991

Commercial Appeal, "High Profile," by Paul Turner, February 28, 1988

Communique, Michigan State University College of Osteopathic Medicine, Summer 1997, Fall 1998, Fall 2004, Summer 2005

Cortlandt Forum: A Physician's Forum for the Exchange of Ideas, 7/96, 10/98, 1/00, 8/00, 3/01, 1/02, 4/02

Delta Business Journal, November 1999, February 2000

Diocesan News, by *Mississippi Catholic*, November 24, 2015

DMU Magazine, Summer 2008

DO, 6/1986, 2/1992, 3/1992, 10/1993, 9/1995, 4/1998, 7/2000, 9/2002, 12/2004, 5/2006, 8/2006, 7/2008, 8/2008

Excellence in Medicine Awards, American Medical Association Foundation, 2005

Extension: The Magazine of Mission America, May/June 1994, November 1987, October 1988, December 1992, May/June 1994, January 1996, October 1997, June 2003, November 2003, November 2007

Faith & Culture: The Magazine of the Pope John Paul UU Cultural Center, Spring 2005

50 Plus, "The Healing of Soul and Body" by Les Lindeman, December 1987
Florida Catholic, September 16, 1994
Humane Medicine: A Journal of the Art and Science of Medicine, vol. 7, no. 4, October 1991
International Journal of the W. K. Kellogg Foundation, volume 3, number 1
People, "Sister Anne Brooks, Doctor and Nun, Practices without Preaching to the Poor" by Bill Shaw, March 23, 1987
Spokesman Review, May 10, 1993
Tutwiler Clinic and Outreach Newsletter, Spring, Summer, Fall, 2000–2017

Unpublished Resources
Anne Brooks's private papers and journals
An interview with Dr. Brooks by Helen Meldrum Bentley College, 2007

Selected Books
I Believe in Love, Fr. Jean C. J. D'Elbée
Sister in Arms, Jo Ann Kay McNamara
How Nuns Work, Molly Edmonds.
Mississippi: A History, Wesley F. Busbee Jr.

Internet
Copies of the two *60 Minutes* programs are in the archives of the Tutwiler Clinic at www.tutwilerclinic.org.
Wikipedia articles were relied upon for basic background on Tallahatchie County, the history of Tutwiler, the history of the Catholic Church, Pope Leo XIII, Pope John Paul XXIII, and the history of Order of the Sisters of the Holy Names of Jesus and Mary, plus their website at www.snjm.org.
In researching Sister Anne's family background these sites were used:
Ancestry.com—Brooks and Goebels census reports, marriage records, etc.
Archives.com—Roger Brooks's service records
Newspapers.com—obituary of Prof. Goebel
E-Yearbook.com—University of Illinois 1916–1920, Naval Academy 1920
Swarthmore.edu—Finding aid for Brooks Family Papers, 1790–1992 RG5/252

INDEX

ABOUT THE AUTHORS

Sally Palmer Thomason was born, raised, and educated in California but has lived in Memphis for over fifty years. She retired as the dean of continuing and corporate education at Rhodes College and has authored four books, including *Delta Rainbow: The Irrepressible Betty Bobo Pearson*, published by the University Press of Mississippi.

Jean Carter Fisher is a licensed clinical social worker at Lakeside Behavioral Health System in Memphis, Tennessee, and previously worked at St. Jude Children's Research Hospital. She contributed to *Delta Rainbow: The Irrepressible Betty Bobo Pearson*, published by the University Press of Mississippi.